CW00733592

The Sustainable Procurement Guide

Procuring sustainably using BS 8903

Cathy Berry

First published in the UK in 2011
by
BSI
389 Chiswick High Road
London W4 4AL

© British Standards Institution 2011

All rights reserved. Except as permitted under the *Copyright, Designs and Patents Act 1988*, no part of this publication may be reproduced, stored in a retrieval system or transmitted in any form or by any means – electronic, photocopying, recording or otherwise – without prior permission in writing from the publisher.

Whilst every care has been taken in developing and compiling this publication, BSI accepts no liability for any loss or damage caused, arising directly or indirectly in connection with reliance on its contents except to the extent that such liability may not be excluded in law.

While every effort has been made to trace all copyright holders, anyone claiming copyright should get in touch with the BSI at the above address.

BSI has no responsibility for the persistence or accuracy of URLs for external or third-party internet websites referred to in this book, and does not guarantee that any content on such websites is, or will remain, accurate or appropriate.

The right of Cathy Berry to be identified as the author of this Work has been asserted by her in accordance with sections 77 and 78 of the *Copyright, Designs and Patents Act 1988*.

Typeset in Frutiger by Helius – www.helius.biz
Printed in Great Britain by Berforts Group – www.berforts.co.uk

British Library Cataloguing in Publication Data
A catalogue record for this book is available from the British Library

ISBN 978-0-580-69861-3

Contents

Contents

Contents

Contents

Foreword

This book, and the accompanying guidance, BS 8903, is all about trying to translate between procurement and sustainability language to make unfamiliar concepts and terms work in a way we can understand. This is quite a task. Procurement professionals tend to use quite precise language, with objective tender evaluations, precise contract clauses and regimented performance and risk management programmes. Sustainability is contextual and will vary between organizations as they take a different view of how their business interacts with the society and environment around them. For example, the world faces the universal problem of climate change. According to most scientists the world is warming at a rate that will ultimately limit the ability of the human race to survive on earth. This is coupled with an exponential rise in the population and industrialization of countries with massive populations such as India, China and Brazil, leading to more emissions and a strain on finite natural resources. There is also a constant dilemma of global or local sourcing; procurement people have spent decades chasing the money in a global search for cheaper labour and materials. On the other hand, organizations with a high level of interaction with their local community such as local authorities or businesses with a local impact such as developers or operators of public infrastructure have a desire to see more business done with the communities in which they operate. For the procurement professional it feels like they are being asked to solve world peace and hunger with no help or guidance about how to do it.

This book will not solve world peace and hunger, but makes a humble attempt to demystify sustainability for procurement professionals. It takes these global concepts, sets out how these can be translated into business objectives and delivered through a supply chain. We have also set out some case studies and examples of good practice to follow. It is inevitably a snapshot in time, dealing with issues as we see them in 2011. Having taken on board the concepts in this book, it is important for the reader to keep up to date with the issues which change rapidly, as our society changes and as we start to understand more about our impact on the environment.

As far as we are aware, this is the first book of its kind marking a new era for sustainable procurement and creating a common language and understanding. It represents collaboration between the author, Cathy Berry aided (and sometimes confused) by myself and my old friend and mentor Martin Sykes. In spite of our efforts to baffle her with our random input, Cathy has done a wonderful job of creating a book which provides straightforward guidance to clarify a subject that is much misunderstood by procurement people. We are also very grateful to the numerous people who provided case studies, model solutions and anecdotes that make it an interesting read.

Cathy's time writing this book was generously given by Action Sustainability CIC, a social enterprise that I am proud to be a director of. Martin and I have given our time for free. Any royalties received from the sale of the book will be used by Action Sustainability CIC to further the body of knowledge related to sustainable business.

Shaun McCarthy
Director, Action Sustainability CIC Ltd
Chair, Commission for a Sustainable London 2012

About the author

Cathy Berry has over 12 years' supply chain experience in leading international companies. Her previous role was Supply Chain Risk and Governance Manager for British Airports Authority (BAA), responsible for developing and reporting supply chain risk management strategy, staff capability development and improving supply chain processes to embed risk methodologies. Prior to this Cathy spent 6 years as a procurement consultant gaining significant experience across a range of industry sectors, including pharmaceuticals, telecoms and FMCG. Cathy joined Action Sustainability in 2009 and has primarily been focused on working with the BS 8903 committee drafting the sustainable procurement guidance standard.

Action Sustainability is a not-for-profit social enterprise registered as a Community Interest Company. Set up in 2006, initially funded by Defra through the Business Resource Efficiency and Waste Programme, Action Sustainability's aim is to continuously extend, lead and inspire sustainable procurement, by extending the boundaries of best practice.

www.actionsustainability.com

1. Sustainable procurement: an overview

Introduction

Sustainability is a broad concept examining how societies live, interact and operate. It means trying to find ways for humankind to live, work and play that do not interfere with nature's inherent ability to sustain life. It considers our economic, social and environmental needs and involves taking responsibility for the local, regional and global impacts of our way of life. It also requires that we take a longer-term view when making decisions to ensure meeting our own needs does not compromise the needs of others both today and for future generations.

We now have greater understanding of the impacts of human activity on our environment. We recognize that if we carry on living the way we do and change nothing, then the impacts will be beyond what the planet can currently support. While consumption and pollution varies widely between regions, if everyone lived as we do in the UK we would need three planets' worth of resources to support us.[1] Sustainability is about acknowledging that we need to learn to live within a fair share of the earth's resources and changing our behaviours to enable us to so. It is also about everybody's right to be treated with respect and enjoy a decent standard of living.

Sustainability is fundamentally about people, how we live and the choices that we make to find the balance between economic, social and environmental needs. Finding this balance is not quick or easy. We are all on a 'journey', with some individuals, organizations or nations ahead of others in terms of making this transition to a more sustainable way of living. This 'journey' may be described using four basic elements, as outlined below.

First is *awareness*. In the UK and across Europe we are being informed by the media on a daily basis of the consequences of climate change, our consumption patterns and the need to reassess our lifestyles for the good of humankind. The concepts around sustainability are generally known; for example, we know that it is a bad idea to waste natural resources or pollute the environment, and we are becoming aware of the need for local self-sufficiency using sustainable sources of energy, food and other resources. However, this is not the case across the world; even in the USA such issues receive far less publicity. Some developing nations for many years have seen climate change as a plan hatched by the West to limit their ability to create wealth and raise living standards. However, over the past few years awareness and acceptance of the issues at a global level has increased. There is a growing recognition that all societies must play a part and take action to avoid irreversible degradation of our planet.

Another element is *understanding*. Leaders, governments and organizations at all levels need to lead by example, promote understanding and show people why and how to make more sustainable choices.

Behaviour change is essential. Those in leadership roles need to sustain the momentum for change and incentivize and empower individuals to follow suit. We need to provide people with sustainable alternatives to allow them to make optimum choices for themselves and for wider society. Global collective action is required to tackle some of the more complex sustainability challenges such as climate change and this will take vision, courage and leadership.

The final element is to *make a difference and affect change*. For example, a global construction contractor has a scheme to employ ex-offenders. This involves an element of risk for the company but they find that they generally balance the risk with the benefits of recruiting loyal workers who tend to stay with the company, reducing the cost of re-recruitment. Society wins because the rate of reoffending reduces radically and the individual wins with a more prosperous and stable life. A company building care homes is developing a site with a nursery, a doctor's surgery and an energy centre based on waste and biomass; the site also has land set aside for food growing, with the residents able to do so, participating in growing their own food and the children in the nursery learning about how food is grown. All of these elements are profitable for the company, and self-sufficiency in energy reduces fuel costs and attracts government grants. The elderly residents have ready access to medical care through the doctor's surgery. It is well demonstrated that elderly people fare better when they have access to children and green space, so everybody wins. These 'virtuous cycles' of sustainability have no losers, but examples are rare. Organizations and the people in them need to think and behave differently in order to make a difference.

Organizations have a major role to play in this transition. Sustainable business practices are rapidly evolving and we are continually learning and improving. New technologies are emerging which are not only economically viable but create social and environmental benefits. Organizations need to embrace this transition and demonstrate leadership at all levels.

The increasing importance of corporate social responsibility (CSR) within organizations reflects this transition. Over the last decade CSR has moved from something done by a separate function, typically involving single-issue initiatives on the edge of business, to something much more integral to an organization's core operation. A responsible organization will treat its people well, will look after its customers and will be interested in supporting its local communities and those of its supply chains. CSR forms part of this organization's DNA.

In the same way a buyer's role has also evolved. Purchasing goods, works and services, efficiently, with minimum risk and at the best possible value remain central elements of the job. However, buyers must now also consider 'value' in a broader way. They must also consider the additional risks (and opportunities), including the ethical, social and environmental impacts of what they buy. This goes even further. Buyers must also consider the impacts on the supply chain of *how* they buy and operate. Shortening lead times and purchase prices may seem like a good business strategy, but not at the expense of labour standards further down the supply chain or the risk to your reputation due to worker exploitation.

Sustainable procurement goals

Sir Neville Simms, chairman of the government's Sustainable Procurement Task Force,[2] summed up the concept of sustainable procurement as 'using procurement to support wider economic, social and environmental objectives in ways that offer real long-term benefits'. Sustainable procurement attempts to achieve a competitive, responsible and enduring approach to procuring goods, works and services. It is not an abstract, idealistic goal but a practical and achievable objective for organizations large and small.

Sustainable procurement has four main aims:

1 To minimize any negative impacts of goods, works or services across their life cycle and through the supply chain (e.g. impacts on health and well-being, air quality, generation and disposal of hazardous waste).
2 To minimize demand for resources. (Remember the most sustainable produce is the one that we never buy at all!) (For example, reducing purchases, using resource-efficient products such as energy-efficient appliances, fuel-efficient vehicles and products containing recycled content.)

3 To ensure that fair contract prices and terms are applied and respected that meet minimum ethical, human rights and employment standards.
4 To promote diversity and equality throughout the supply chain. Supply chains should aim to reflect the diversity and demographics of the societies that they touch and should provide opportunities for small- and medium-sized businesses (SMEs) and voluntary sector organizations. Sustainable procurement should also support training and skills development. In summary, sustainable procurement should attempt to minimize negative outcomes and promote positive outcomes for the economy, environment and society.

About this book

Many practitioners understand what sustainable procurement is but there is still a lot of confusion around how to implement this. This book aims to be a comprehensive guide to sustainable procurement providing clear, practical advice on how to approach sustainable procurement issues and how to embed these practices within an organization.

The next three chapters provide a foundation or background around the concept of sustainability. This begins with a basic introduction to 'sustainable development', i.e. what it means, what the key issues are and why we need to act. It also examines the complex subject of promoting behaviour change and the differing degrees of sustainability ambition demonstrated by organizations. Chapter 3 examines what sustainable procurement is, the basic principles and takes a more detailed look at the social, economic and environmental issues. Chapter 4 considers 'why' organizations are taking sustainable procurement seriously and looks at the key business drivers of sustainable procurement.

Chapter 5 summarizes the British standard for sustainable procurement (BS 8903). This standard explores how sustainable outcomes fit within procurement priorities. Buyers must understand this in relation to their own organizations' business objectives. This chapter summarizes all the main clauses detailed in BS 8903 which include the sustainability considerations that should be addressed across a generic procurement process.

The latter chapters of this book tackle some of the more challenging issues faced by buyers when buying goods and services. These issues have been chosen in response to the questions most frequently posed to Action Sustainability[3] by its clients. These chapters attempt to provide some clear and practical guidance to enable buyers to feel confident when tackling such issues. The questions explored in this book are:

- How far down the supply chain should I go? (When assessing risk and sustainability.)
- Does sustainable procurement cost more?
- What tools and techniques should I use to promote sustainable outcomes?
- Standards, codes of practice and auditing – are these enough to assure sustainability in your supply chain?
- How do I measure sustainable procurement performance?

The concluding chapter of this book discusses the need to promote continuous learning and sharing within and across organizations. It also takes a look at how sustainability may evolve in future.

BS 8903 – The British standard for sustainable procurement

BS 8903 *Principles and framework for procuring sustainably* was first published in August 2010. It is not a specification standard but a guidance standard, which means the clauses are precisely that – for guidance. Procurement processes and practices vary across organizations and sectors. It is not realistic or practical to 'specify' exactly how sustainable procurement should be included within an organization's business processes and strategy. This requires judgement and this standard is intended to help managers and buyers include sustainable considerations when making purchasing decisions that support their business strategy.

The standard is divided into three areas:

1. What is sustainable procurement?
2. Why practise sustainable procurement?
3. How to do sustainable procurement.

The initial chapters of this book build on the first two areas listed above. It discusses the concepts in more depth and illustrates the issues with practical examples. However, the majority of the standard is dedicated to providing guidance in the third area. Figure 1 provides a pictorial overview of the key elements discussed which are classified as:

> Fundamentals – these are the higher-level organizational and procurement policies and strategies that should be in place to provide the strategic context and strategic priorities to guide sustainable procurement practices and decision making.
> Procurement process – BS 8903 follows a generic procurement process and identifies the sustainability considerations and activities that should be addressed at various points across this process.
> Enablers – these include ways of working, competencies, practices and techniques that should be in place and utilized by managers or buyers on an ongoing or periodic basis. These enablers *support* the activities within the procurement process.

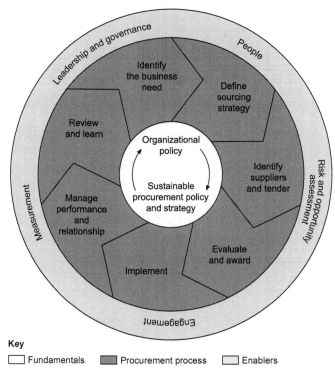

Key
☐ Fundamentals   ▨ Procurement process   ☐ Enablers

Figure 1 – Sustainable procurement process overview

This book is not intended to be a duplication and build of BS 8903. As such Chapter 5 summarizes the key information outlined by the fundamentals, enablers and process. However, it will provide some practical examples to show how organizations are employing techniques or practices. The latter half of the book then discusses some elements within the procurement process that often cause confusion or are cited by buyers as areas where clear and practical guidance would be helpful.

Useful resources

BS 8903 *Principles and framework for procuring sustainably – Guide.*

References

1   Taken from the One Planet Initiative, see www.bioregional.com
2   Sustainable Procurement Task Force, 'Procuring the Future', Foreword, p.1, see www.defra.gov.uk/sustainable/government/documents/full-document.pdf
3   Action Sustainability is a not-for-profit social enterprise specializing in delivering sustainable procurement consultancy and business support across the UK, see: www.actionsustainability.com

2. Sustainable development: the wider context

Introduction

This chapter explores the wider issue of sustainable development: what it means, what the important issues are and how we can promote behaviour change to actually make a difference. The final part of this chapter looks at sustainability aspirations specifically within organizations. It examines the differing levels of ambition towards driving real change and generating more sustainable service delivery, business solutions and lifestyle choices.

What is sustainable development and why is it important?

The most often quoted definition of sustainable development is:

> development that meets the needs of the present without compromising the ability of future generations to meet their needs.[1]

Meeting the needs of the present means ensuring both social and economic well-being within viable environmental limits so that future generations can also attain a decent standard of living and quality of life. There is a growing recognition that we are currently living beyond our means, the planet on which we depend is finite and the burden we are placing on it is unsustainable.

> Our economic system – our civilization – is only possible if the basic resources of the atmosphere, oceans, forests and soils and fundamental processes like the climate system and its carbon and hydrological cycles remain intact. To make economics and ecology into enemies is to doom both.
>
> New Copenhagen Climate Deal WWF[2]

We must create a development model that promotes strong, sustainable communities and that balances production and consumption within environmental limits. To do this it is possible that we need to overturn some

---

of the received learning on procurement, to reverse some of the globalization, some of the aggregation, and move to more local sourcing and co-production in order to achieve sustainable communities. This isn't necessarily counter to the big picture: for example, emphasis on more local production might have a positive impact on our carbon footprint and lead to more reuse and recycling. (However this does leave us with another conundrum which is the potential impact on third-world communities if we reduce imports of their products.)

The realization that our current development model is unsustainable has been emerging over the past 25 years. *Our Common Future*, first published in 1987 by the United Nations World Commission on Environment and Development (WCED), placed environmental issues firmly on the political agenda and aimed to bring the environment and development as one single issue.

The key *environmental* issues arising from the burden humans are placing on the planet can be summarized as:[3]

- resource depletion and the increasing stress on environmental systems – water, land and air – from the way we produce, consume and waste resources;
- biodiversity loss across ecosystems from rainforests to fish stocks; and
- climate change and its consequences.

Our way of life has also led to great *social* inequality in human health, education and wealth around the world. For example:

- In 2009 an estimated 1.02 billion people were undernourished, a sizeable increase from the 2006 estimate of 854 million (United Nations Food and Agriculture Organization).[4]
- Almost half the world – over 3 billion people – live on less than $2.50[5] per day.
- 884 million people in the world do not have access to safe water. This is roughly one in eight of the world's population (WHO/UNICEF).[6]
- 2.5 billion people do not have access to adequate sanitation; this is almost two-fifths of the world's population (WHO/UNICEF).[6]
- 1.4 million children die every year from diarrhoea caused by unclean water and poor sanitation, i.e. one child in every 20 (WHO/UNICEF).[6]
- UNESCO estimates that 847 million people over the age of 15 were illiterate in 2010.[7]

To ensure human well-being globally, we all need access to adequate natural resources and a healthy environment. Sustainable development is about shifting to a more sustainable, fairer future in which all people and nature can thrive. These inequalities aren't limited to overseas. They are also evident across the UK, for example:

- The Joseph Rowntree Foundation estimated in 2006–7 that 75,000 young people experienced homelessness in the UK.[8]
- In 2009, 13.4 million people were living in low-income households, the highest level since 2000 and the number of people living below 40 per cent of the median income – that is, those with the very lowest incomes – is now higher than at any point in the last 25 years.[9]
- 2009 NHS Health figures show the gap in life expectancy between the prosperous middle classes and those in the most deprived homes is widening. Messages about well-being and healthier lifestyles are getting through to middle-class professional households, while the poorer are not responding; they are still drinking and smoking and cannot afford to change diets.[10]
- Men in Blackpool are living on average up to 73.2 years, 10.5 years fewer than men living in Kensington and Chelsea. Women in Hartlepool have the lowest female life expectancy at 78.1 years, which is 9.6 years fewer than in Kensington and Chelsea.[10]

A more detailed look at the issues

In 2005 the UK government published *Securing the Future* a report setting out its sustainable development strategy. This report outlined five key principles and four sustainable development priorities for the UK. The principles are set out in Figure 2. These provide the strategic approach to guide the four priority areas for action.

The four priorities for UK action were identified as:

1 sustainable communities;
2 sustainable consumption and production;
3 natural resource protection and environmental enhancement; and
4 climate change and energy.

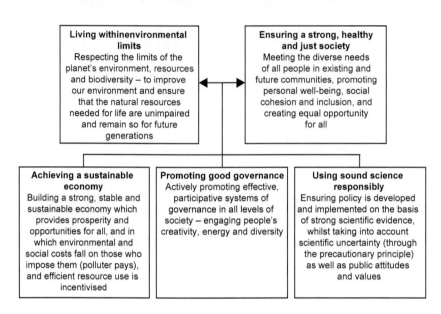

Figure 2 – Five key principles of sustainable development
(© Crown Copyright 2005, *Securing the Future*)

Creating sustainable communities and a fairer world

Creating Sustainable Communities means putting sustainable development into practice. Sustainable Communities must combine social inclusion, homes, jobs, services, infrastructure and respect for the environment to create places where people will want to live and work now and in the future.

Rt Hon. John Prescott MP, Deputy Prime Minister, February 2005

- At the *local level* this involves improving people's lives by delivering better neighbourhoods; cleaner, safer, greener, healthier communities; homes for all and promoting stronger neighbourhood engagement.
- At the *national level* this means ensuring opportunities for all including the most disadvantaged and most vulnerable groups in society. For example, some cities within the UK are experiencing third-generation economic

inactivity and are struggling with the consequences on health and crime that such a lack of employment prospects can bring.
- At the *global level* this means tackling the major social, economic and environmental inequalities.

Inequality across the world is stark, for example, the poorest 40 per cent of the world's population accounts for 5 per cent of global income while the richest 20 per cent accounts for three-quarters of world income.[11]

Global inequality in consumption levels is also marked. In 2005, the wealthiest 20 per cent of the world accounted for 76.6 per cent of total private consumption. The poorest 20 per cent of the world's population consumed just 1.5 per cent. (See Figure 3.)

Tackling such inequalities at all levels is central to creating a fairer world. Long-term growth is dependent on a thriving global community and environment. This means we have to reconsider the relationship between ethical and economic goals which are too often perceived as opposing choices.

Organizations can make a real difference. Positive action at a community level such as investing in community projects, engaging with local businesses, improving the employment prospects of long-term unemployed through skills development, work experience and training, and providing opportunities for

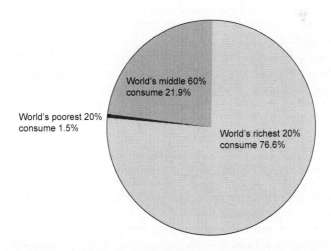

Figure 3 – Share of world's private consumption 2005

apprenticeships are just a few examples. The procurement choices organizations make can also affect real change for the individuals and communities affected by its supply chains. Professor Angie Hobbs indicates that organizations may have to sacrifice some short-term profits, but by taking an ethical and sustainable approach, there are more gains to be achieved in the long term. For instance, trustworthy companies will attract the best graduates, and shareholders are increasingly demanding ethical stewardship in addition to return on investments.[12]

> Do your little bit of good where you are; it's those little bits of good put together that overwhelm the world.
>
> Archbishop Desmond Tutu

This issue should not just be directed at the nation's leaders or its organizations. We are all citizens and each day we have the opportunity to make choices that can have a positive impact on society, the economy and the environment – no matter how small. Remember that each time we spend our money we also cast a vote for the type of world we want to live in.

Sustainable consumption and production

This means using less resources and making things efficiently. We need to work out how to satisfy our needs in ways that do not negatively impact the environment and wider society. This will require us all to have a better understanding about the impacts of our choices and for more sustainable alternatives to be made available. Increasing prosperity in the UK and globally has allowed us to enjoy the benefits of goods and services that were once only available to a few and as a result we are now consuming too much. In summary we must break the cycle of economic growth at the expense of the natural environment, become more resource efficient and understand the impacts of products and materials across their whole life cycle.

For organizations, improving production efficiencies means using less resources; this saves money and boosts competitiveness. Organizations also need to be concerned about how and where things are made to ensure that neither the environment nor the communities producing their goods and services are being exploited therefore ensuring the reputation of the organization is not put at risk. This issue links directly to sustainable procurement which attempts to drive responsible practice throughout the supply chain which supports social, economic and environmental objectives.

At a global level, consumption continues to rise due to spectacular economic growth in some developing countries, improvements in living standards and a rapidly increasing global population. Figure 4 demonstrates how global population has more than doubled in under 50 years.

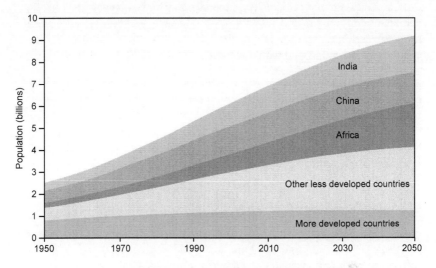

Figure 4 – World population growth
(2008 World Population Data Sheet
www.prb.org/pdf08/08WPDS_Eng.pdf)

Natural resource protection and environmental enhancement

Natural resources are vital to our existence. Our health and well-being are inextricably linked to the quality of our air, water, soils and biological resources. Our economy and key industrial sectors rely directly and indirectly upon these natural resources and functioning ecosystems.

The world's ecosystems are complex and integrated; therefore degrading one aspect of the natural environment has consequences across many ecosystems. We need to understand the impact of our actions and ensure that economic development occurs while ensuring our natural resources are protected and enhanced.

Resources such as biodiversity and soils are typically thought of as 'renewable' but they can be exploited to the extent that long-term irreversible damage occurs. These renewables must therefore be managed within their environmental limits. For example, vast swathes of pristine rainforest across South-East Asia have been cleared using slash-and-burn methods to make way for palm oil plantations. The degradation of these critical ecosystems is irreversible, and they are also critical to the survival of orang-utan populations which some sources have indicated could be extinct in the wild within ten years.[13]

In summary an integrated approach to development is required which considers ecosystems as a whole taking into account social, economic and environmental objectives. We should strive to achieve social, economic and environmental development where the improvement of one is not to the detriment of another. If and where competing objectives are unavoidable, any decisions should be transparent and minimize negative impacts.

Climate change and energy

Climate change is perhaps the greatest single consequence of unsustainability and its effects can already be seen. Temperatures and sea levels are rising, ice and snow cover is declining and fragile ecosystems are being damaged, including coral reefs, the Amazon rainforest and the Arctic. Climate change is already contributing to severe droughts, floods and hurricanes and increasing the spread of diseases such as malaria and dengue fever. If left unchecked, the consequences for the natural world and society could be catastrophic.

There are some who are still sceptical about the causes of climate change. However, the Intergovernmental Panel on Climate Change (IPCC),[14] which is the leading body for the assessment of climate change, in its fourth assessment report in 2007 stated climate change is happening and is 'unequivocal'. It also stated that global average temperature rises since the mid-twentieth century is 'very likely' due to human-induced rises in greenhouse gas (GHG) concentrations.[15]

The Climate Change Act was enacted in November 2008 and makes the UK the first country in the world to have a legally binding long-term framework to cut carbon emissions. The target of at least an 80 per cent cut in GHG emissions by

2050 is to be achieved through action in the UK and abroad. Also a reduction in emissions of at least 34 per cent by 2020 must be achieved. Both these targets are against a 1990 baseline.

However, a common, global agreement on climate change is still needed. The first commitment period of the Kyoto Protocol ends in 2012 and while negotiations at the United Nations Climate Change Conference in Copenhagen in December 2009 did not agree the next framework for an international agreement to reduce GHG emissions, some progress has been made and it is likely to be only a matter of time until this is achieved.

Promoting behaviour change

Information does not necessarily lead to increased awareness, and increased awareness does not necessarily lead to action.

Demos and Green Alliance, 2003

Helping people, businesses and societies to make better choices to achieve sustainable development and sustainable living is a complex issue. Information alone does not lead to behaviour change. This section explores a behaviour change model which has been based on research about what influences the way we choose.[16]

This model uses a number of levers and focuses on the need to *enable*, *exemplify*, *encourage* and *engage* people and communities in the move towards sustainability. This was published in *Securing the Future* and has been used by the government to help deliver its sustainable development strategy. The main point is that a range of actions, approaches and information is required simultaneously. Any approach must be comprehensive and consistent with credible messages and actions to exemplify any changes required. Figure 5 illustrates this model.

This figure set outs the elements the government could employ using the four approaches, *enable*, *encourage*, *engage* and *exemplify* and the various elements under each of these approaches. While these elements are all deemed necessary for change to take place they may not be sufficient to bring about change when behaviour is entrenched. In these circumstances further policies or approaches

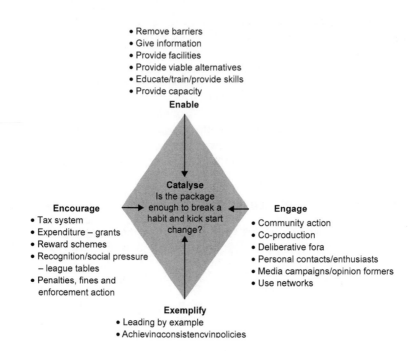

Figure 5 – Behaviour change model
(© Crown Copyright 2005, *Securing the Future*)

may be needed to *catalyze* people to think differently. London's congestion charge provides an example of how this model can work in practice. A combination of charging, combined with increased provision of buses was introduced with a huge amount of publicity. It has been hugely successful with a 30 per cent reduction in congestion as people consider alternatives including public transport with an increase of 29,000 bus passengers entering the zone in the morning peak.

How sustainability ambitions vary across organizations

Organizations have a key role to play in promoting behaviour change. Implementation of sustainable business practices and provision of sustainable solutions, sustainable products and services help to improve understanding and awareness throughout the supply chain and provide the consumer with alternative choices. However, the level of commitment to sustainable business practices and corporate social responsibility (CSR) varies markedly between organizations. Significant progress has been made and CSR has moved up the management agenda over the past ten years; nevertheless we still have some way to go before CSR commitments receive the same level of attention as financial performance, productivity, new business pipelines, etc.

CSR considers how companies should manage their business processes to produce a positive impact on society. Sustainability expert Shaun McCarthy indicates that there are 'few rules' to CSR and companies tend to 'set their own ambitions based on their perception of the market and their stakeholders'. These can typically be divided into four groups based on the amount of research done to consider objectives and the level of ambition set (Figure 6):[17]

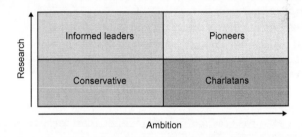

Figure 6 – Four approaches to CSR

1 Pioneers – these companies research well and then set very stretching targets. These tend to be businesses that perceive significant competitive advantage in being more sustainable, sometimes a long way into the future.
2 Informed leaders – these companies research well and set achievable targets. These tend to be companies for whom the risk of failure is high and public trust is important. Utility companies and others managing public infrastructure would be a good example of this.
3 Conservative – these companies do not see a compelling reason to be leaders and tend to be followers; they will look at trends in the market, what their competitors and peers are doing and set objectives accordingly. These objectives tend to be conservative and achievable.
4 Charlatans – companies setting ambitious targets based on little or no research, usually to gain a quick win or to score expedient political points. Statements such as 'visionary', 'carbon neutral' or some words starting with 'eco' might appear in such mission statements.

There is no right or wrong approach. The approach must be in the context of your business:

- Pioneers tend to have a good reason to take this approach; this may be driven by a perceived strong competitive advantage, like Marks & Spencer, extreme risk, such as the reputation risk in the sportswear sector, or investment in long-term growth, like the GE Ecomagination (http://ge.ecomagination.com/) programme.
- Informed leaders often have a long-term investment to protect, often in public infrastructure or services; they have a responsibility to be sustainable but there is a high risk or limited return from a more ambitious approach. United Utilities (www.unitedutilities.com/crreport.htm), nominated Business in the Community Company of the Year in 2009, is a good example of this.
- Conservative target setters will often differentiate themselves around something other than sustainability (price, speed to market, quality, etc.) and need sustainability as a supporting strategy.
- While a Charlatan approach is not recommended here, it is legitimate provided it is legal and does not mislead people.

To summarize, the context of any business is set by its stakeholders. These may be customers or employees (now or in the future), shareholders, competitors, government bodies, non-government organizations and many others. Each company will have a unique set of drivers which will dictate the approach.

Learning summary

In summary, sustainable development requires an integrated approach which takes account of social, economic and environmental objectives. This also means trying to ensure that the advancement of one objective is not to the detriment of another. Climate change may be seen as the most prominent, single issue requiring co-ordination and leadership at a global level; however, we also need to recognize that our choices and actions at all levels – individual, organizations and society – can also make a difference. The sustainable development challenges that we face are not just down to national leaders to deal with; behaviour change is needed at all levels and we all must play our part and affect what we can no matter how seemingly small or insignificant.

There is no one-size-fits-all approach to achieving sustainability and at an organizational level this should be set within the context of your business.

There are many business reasons for an organization to become sustainability focused and these are explored in more detail in the next chapter.

Useful resources

Securing the Future, UK Government Sustainable Development Strategy, 2005. See: www.defra.gov.uk/sustainable/government/publications/uk-strategy/

Poverty, Inequality and Policy Since 1997, John Hill, Tom Sefton and Kitty Stewart. Joseph Rowntree Foundation, see: www.jrf.org.uk/publications/poverty-inequality-and-policy-1997

London's Quality of Life Indicators. 2008–9 report. London Sustainable Development Commission. See www.londonsdc.org/documents/qol_reports/QoL_indicators.pdf

'Five Ways to Wellbeing: The Evidence. The New Economics Foundation', October 2008; see: www.neweconomics.org/publications/five-ways-well-being-evidence

'The key to tackling health inequalities'. Sustainable Development' Commission 2010. See: www.sd-commission.org.uk/publications/downloads/health_inequalities.pdf

Climate Change

Climate Change 2007: Synthesis Report. IPCC Fourth Assessment Report (AR4) see www.ipcc.ch/publications_and_data/publications_ipcc_fourth_assessment_report_synthesis_report.htm

Stern Review on the Economics of Climate Change. October 2006. Retrieved from www.hm-treasury.gov.uk/stern_review_report.htm

---

References

1   'Our Common Future' (also known as the Bruntland report). United Nations World Commission on Environment and Development (WCED), 1987.

---

2   *The New Copenhagen Climate Deal: A Pocket Guide*. First edition published in May 2009 by WWF-World Wide Fund for Nature (formerly World Wildlife Fund), Gland, Switzerland. This edition, November 2009.

3   *Securing the Future*, ch.1 'A New Strategy', 2005, p.12; see www.defra.gov.uk/sustainable/government/publications/uk-strategy

4   *The State of Food Insecurity in the World 2009. Economic Crises – Impacts and Lessons Learned*. Food and Agriculture Organization of the United Nations, 2009.

5   World Bank Development Indicators 2008, see www.globalissues.org/article/26/poverty-facts-and-stats, plus 'The World Distribution of Household Wealth', Davies, Sandstrom, Shorrocks and Wolff, July 2007, UC Santa Cruz: Center for Global, International and Regional Studies. Retrieved from www.iariw.org/papers/2006/davies.pdf

6   WHO/UNICEF statistics accessed from www.wateraid.org/international/what_we_do/statistics/default.asp

7   UNESCO Institute for Statistics Regional adult illiteracy rate and population gender 1970–2015. International Literacy Day, 8 September 2002. See www.uis.unesco.org/en/stats/statistics/literacy2000.htm

8   'Youth Homelessness in the UK'. Deborah Quilgars, Sarah Johnsen and Nicholas Pleace, 9 May 2008. Retrieved from: www.jrf.org.uk/publications/youth-homelessness-uk

9   Poverty and social exclusion monitoring reports, Joseph Rowntree Foundation, 2009. Retrieved from: www.poverty.org.uk/reports/mpse%202009%20findings.pdf

10 'Life expectancy gap between rich and poor is widening', Owen Bowcott, Guardian.co.uk, 3 July 2009. Retrieved from: www.guardian.co.uk/society/2009/jul/03/life-expectancy-patterns

11 2007 Human Development Report (HDR), United Nations Development Program, 27 November 2007, p.25, www.globalissues.org/article/26/poverty-facts-and-stats#fact3

12 'How to Save and Prosper', *Supply Management*, Emma Clarke, 11 August 2008. Retrieved from: www.supplymanagement.com/analysis/features/2008/how-to-save-and-prosper/?locale=en

13 'Sir David Attenborough calls for more protection for orang-utans', *Daily Telegraph*, 29 April 2009. Retrieved from www.telegraph.co.uk/earth/wildlife/5241749/Sir-David-Attenborough-calls-for-more-protection-for-orang-utans.html

14 The IPCC was established by the United Nations Environment Program (UNEP) and the World Meteorological Organization (WMO) to provide the

world with a clear view on the current state of climate change and its potential consequences.

15 Climate Change 2007: Synthesis Report. IPCC Fourth Assessment Report (AR4) see www.ipcc.ch/publications_and_data/publications_ipcc_fourth_assessment_report_synthesis_report.htm

16 *Securing the Future*, 2005, ch.2 pp.25–6, 'Helping People Make Better Choices', see www.defra.gov.uk/sustainable/government/publications/uk-strategy/

17 'CSR Ambitions'. Shaun McCarthy, October 2009. Retrieved from www.actionsustainability.com/news/221/CSR-ambitions/

3. What is sustainable procurement?

Introduction

The focus of this chapter is sustainable procurement; how it can be defined, the associated issues and the general principles. The terms ethical procurement, responsible procurement, environmental procurement or 'green' procurement are all terms widely used to describe this subject. However, we should use the term 'sustainable' to adequately reflect the goal of providing benefits to society, the environment and the economy through procurement. These three elements are also referred to as the three pillars of sustainable procurement and the latter part of this chapter takes a more detailed look at the social, economic and environmental issues in relation to procurement.

What is sustainable procurement?

Sustainable procurement is still an emerging area and the sustainability agenda continues to evolve as our understanding and competence to deal with the issues and opportunities improve. Supply Management have a history of polls which reflect this growing understanding; in November 2006 it found that 86 per cent of buyers polled did not have a clear understanding of the term sustainable procurement.[1] The following year the same poll showed a significant improvement with 55 per cent of buyers polled now having a clear understanding of the term.[2]

However, there is no single, universally accepted definition. This is partly because it is a relatively new concept and also because the application of sustainable procurement differs between both organizations and sectors. The most regularly cited definition is:

> Sustainable procurement is a process whereby organizations meet their needs for goods, service, works or utilities in a way that achieves value for money on a whole of life basis in terms of generating benefits not only to the organization, but also to society and the economy, while minimizing damage to the environment.
>
> *Procuring the Future*[3]

Another useful definition is offered by Sir Neville Simms, chairman of the Sustainable Procurement Task Force: 'using procurement to support wider economic, social and environmental objectives in ways that offer real long term value'.[3]

The definitions above emphasize the need to use procurement to benefit the environment, society *and* the economy. This means purchasers need to look beyond the conventional criteria of price, quality and service when making purchasing decisions with a view to maximizing benefits for themselves and the wider world.

> The message … is simple: this is worth doing, there are clear benefits, it can be done, it is not difficult.
>
> Sir Neville Simms, *Procuring the Future*[3]

Sustainable procurement should consider the relationship between economic and ethical goals. It is about finding the right balance between the issues. Often these goals are perceived as opposing ideals as though a choice must be made between the two. This is a false distinction. Organizations may need to sacrifice some short-term profits but by taking a sustainable approach, there are frequently more gains that can be achieved in the medium or longer term. Figure 7 a) shows how sustainable procurement attempts to find the balance between these goals.

Figure 7 b) may also be used to illustrate the three pillars of sustainable procurement. While this doesn't demonstrate the need to find balance between sustainable procurement issues, it does show how the pillars relate to one another. For example, economic impacts occur within the overall framework of society. Society in turn exists within, and is wholly dependent on, the environment, which is fundamental to our very existence.

It's important to note that different organizations will place different emphasis on each of the elements in line with overall business objectives. However, even the smallest players have environmental and economic impacts and can offer some support to social issues such as supporting community schemes, offering apprenticeships, or work experience schemes. We also need to recognize that to maximize our contribution will require collaboration; it may also require that participating procurers respect that their own agenda is not the only agenda.

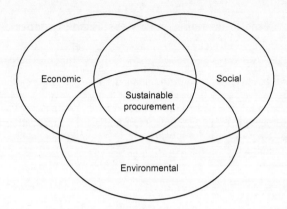

Figure 7 a) – Balancing sustainable procurement objectives

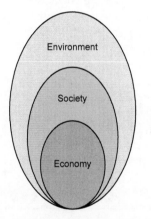

Figure 7 b) – Relationship between the three pillars of sustainable procurement

Others will have different sustainability ambitions and some, none at all. We are ultimately trying to change the behaviours of a magnitude and this will require more of an 'evangelical approach' until all players understand and believe this is the right thing to do so that it becomes embedded into existing processes and routines both professionally and personally.

Table 1 summarizes some of the main issues that are typically captured by the economic, social and environmental pillars of sustainable procurement.

Table 1 – Examples of key sustainability issues

Environmental issues	Social issues	Economic issues
• emissions to air (e.g. greenhouse gases such as carbon dioxide and other pollutants) • releases to water (e.g. chemical pollution of water courses) • releases to land (e.g. chemical fertilizers) • use of raw materials and natural resources (e.g. sustainable forestry, biodiversity) • use of energy (e.g. renewables) • water use • energy emitted (e.g. heat, radiation, vibration, noise) • waste and by-products (e.g. recycling and waste prevention)	• encouraging a diverse base of competitive suppliers (e.g. minority or under-represented suppliers) • promoting fair employment practices (e.g. fair wages, avoidance of bonded labour, workforce equality and diversity) • promoting workforce welfare (e.g. health and safety, freedom to join or form a union) • enabling training opportunities and skills development (e.g. apprenticeships) • community benefits (e.g. supporting community groups, volunteering) • fair trade and ethical sourcing practices (e.g. fair pricing policies)	• job creation (e.g. green technologies, creating markets for recycled products) • whole-life costing • achieving value for money • supporting SMEs (e.g. facilitating opportunities for small businesses) • reducing entry barriers (e.g. facilitating open competition) • Ensuring operating business remains a viable operation able to provide employment • Ensuring suppliers' agreements are competitive and fair to promote business viability

Sustainable procurement principles

BS 8900 Sustainable Development Series Principles

The BS 8900 series is the British standard series covering sustainable development. Each standard uses a common set of principles and values which include *inclusivity*, *integrity*, *stewardship* and *transparency*. While we recognize that principles cannot be imposed on an organization, BS 8900 recommends that its decision making and behaviour should be consistent with these principles. It also indicates that any principles 'should be informed by an organization's

Table 2 – BS 8900 Series Principles

Inclusivity	considering a broad group of stakeholders in decision making and ensuring that no particular groups are disadvantaged
Integrity	encouraging diversity, avoiding corruption and ensuring that decisions and actions are unbiased, and comply with relevant rights, legal obligations and regulations
Stewardship	considering the effects of business decisions on quality of life, the state of the environment and society in general, while developing and sharing sustainable development management skills
Transparency	making sure that relevant and reliable information is available in an accessible, low-cost and comparable way. The reasons for decisions and significant interests, influences or beneficiaries should also be recorded and communicated

Source: BS 8900:2006, *Guidance for managing sustainable development*

values and should relate to commonly held ethical norms that are increasingly reflected in UN and other international agreements covering topics such as human and labour rights, environment and governance'.[4]

Sustainable procurement principles

The principles discussed in the previous section, while relevant to procurement, relate to sustainable development in general. The following set of principles and values relate specifically to sustainable procurement:

- *A sound approach* – sustainable procurement is just good procurement based on fairness, openness and transparency, non-discrimination and competition.
- *An ethical approach* – sustainable procurement should ensure integrity, encourage diversity, avoid corruption and ensure activities comply with International Labour Organization standards for pay and working conditions across the supply chain. This means organizations have an obligation to act ethically and responsibly and look beyond pure economic gain.

- *A holistic approach* – sustainable procurement should consider the effects of procurement decisions on quality of life, the environment and society in general. This also means taking into account the impacts at local, national and international level and requires the whole organization to take responsibility for decision making and outcomes.
- *A risk/opportunity-based approach* – sustainable procurement requires an ongoing process of continual improvement. This means using risk and opportunity assessment to identify and address impacts and solutions at all stages of the product life cycle. Actions should be prioritized in relation to the greatest risks and the greatest opportunities.
- *Leadership* – senior-level leadership is needed for success although leadership can come from all levels within an organization in the form of 'champions'. Buyers should adopt leadership qualities to help build capacity and competence within supply chains and the marketplace. This also involves taking responsibility for decision making to promote sustainable outcomes and a commitment to making a difference wherever appropriate and possible.
- *Delivery of organizational objectives* – sustainable procurement can deliver against a wide range of objectives beyond financial and efficiency savings, from CO_2 emissions savings to innovation strategies.

The environmental context

Environmental concerns remain a key driver behind the sustainable procurement agenda and there is a growing consensus that humanity is placing excessive demands on available resources through unsustainable consumption patterns and lifestyle choices. Sometimes 'green' or environmental procurement is seen as a standalone issue but generally it is now regarded as an integral part of the wider sustainable procurement agenda.

The environmental focus of sustainable procurement has three main themes:

1 *as a way to help mitigate overexploitation of, or damage to, any and all scarce resources* (by ensuring all products are bought from certified sustainable sources and ensuring processing and production techniques are non-polluting);
2 *as a tool to address climate change* (by reducing the amount of carbon expended in the manufacture and delivery of goods and services throughout the supply chain); and

3 *as a means to minimize waste* (by challenging demand, increasing the use of recycled and secondary materials, reducing material use, e.g. reducing disposable packaging and recovering materials at the end of life).

Considering the first theme, which addresses the overexploitation of natural resources, many organizations are now committing to use certified, sustainably sourced materials throughout their supply chain. For example, external stakeholder pressure has led to many global confectionery firms making commitments to buy palm oil from sustainable sources. This is following concern about the impact some palm oil growers are having on the environment as a result of deforestation and destruction of rainforests to make way for palm oil plantations.

A study published by the NHS Sustainable Development Unit in 2008 demonstrates clearly the role procurement can play in the second theme; halting climate change. It examined the sources of its 18 million tonne annual carbon footprint and found that while energy use made up 22 per cent of total emissions, and travel 18 per cent, the other 60 per cent was generated by procurement (defined in this case as the purchase of goods and services through the supply chain by the NHS in England).[5]

The scope of green procurement is broad and can vary from buying stationery from recycled sources to procuring buildings with green roofs that enhance the biodiversity of the area, add insulation to reduce heating in the winter and reduce the need for cooling in summer through the evaporative cooling effect of plants (which also absorb CO_2). Environmentally sound products and supply chains are increasingly being demanded by multiple stakeholders groups, including consumers, shareholders, employees and often by environmental campaigners or pressure groups.

Case study – Environmental pressure groups campaign for greener electronics

Hazardous chemicals such as PVC (vinyl) plastic and brominated flame retardants (BFR) are used in the production of many electronic items. Increasing pressure from external groups has led many electronics companies to make commitments to eliminate use of these chemicals in their product ranges.

PVC contaminates humans and the environment during its production, use and disposal – indeed it is the most environmentally damaging of all plastics, being known to form dioxin, a carcinogen, when burned. Some BFRs do not degrade in the environment and can build up in humans and animals.

Workers – as well as the wider community – who deal with electronic waste are exposed to significant health risks. Burning of electronic waste to recover valuable resources can form dioxins. Eliminating these substances will not only decrease exposure but also increase the recyclability and reusability of electronic products and components.

Environmental considerations have been moving up the agenda of the big electronics organizations over the past few years. This in part is due to pressure from environmental groups who actively publicize the performance of electronics organizations, cutting through any potential 'green wash' and providing consumers with additional environmental information. The *Guide to Greener Electronics* published by Greenpeace is a good example. This guide ranks the 18 top manufacturers of personal computers, mobile phones, TVs and games consoles according to their policies on toxic chemicals, recycling and climate change.

Source: Greenpeace.[6]

Green public procurement

In 2006 the European Council announced its ambition to bring the average level of green public procurement (GPP) in Europe up to the standards being achieved by the best-performing member states by 2010. GPP means contracting authorities take into account environmental elements when procuring goods, works or services at all stages of the project and within the entire life cycle of procured goods.

Public procurement spending amounts to as much as 16 per cent of the EU's gross domestic product, which is a sum equivalent to the GDP of Germany.[7] The intent is that this purchasing power (if used effectively) can drive and shape markets by influencing and incentivizing suppliers to develop new technologies and encouraging more sustainable behaviour. Likewise, the conservation charity WWF published a report in 2009 calling for governments to use more sustainable purchasing policies to drive 'strong home markets for clean energy technology'. Again demonstrating the view that government spending decisions can make a real difference shaping markets and encouraging businesses and consumers to buy more green technology.[8]

See http://ec.europa.eu/environment/gpp/index_en.htm for more information on GPP.

The social context

> Nobody wants their unsustainable behaviour to result in other people suffering.
>
> Monica Saini, London Leaders[9]

Sustainable procurement can also be used as a means to tackle social issues such as inclusiveness, equality, diversity, poverty, unemployment, skills development, regeneration, health and well-being. Many of these issues are interrelated which means a cohesive approach is needed to bring about lasting social improvement. For example, inclusiveness involves breaking down the barriers individuals and communities face; this is closely linked with issues of equality, diversity, poverty and the employment and skills agenda. Another example is deprivation which is a strong determinant of ill health.

Within procurement the social implications are wide ranging. Ten to fifteen years ago social responsibility was typically limited to an organization's concern for the health and safety of its own workforce, possibly extending to tier-one suppliers (i.e. those suppliers who supply goods and services directly, especially if working on site). Today, an organization's social procurement responsibilities can extend to all the individuals and communities involved in, or affected by, the operations of its supply chains. We operate in an increasingly globalized market; supply chains can be long and complex and organizations are recognizing that they must take adequate measures to ensure socially responsible business practices throughout these. The level of rigour applied to the understanding and management of sustainability across supply chains varies markedly between organizations. Some opt to meet minimum legal obligations, others will go further, promoting and monitoring socially responsible business practices, others are being driven by their customers, desire to improve the sustainability of their business operations (and as such are increasingly using the social pillar of sustainable procurement to help to differentiate between potential suppliers). However, sustainability leaders will proactively drive change with the intention of really improving the lives of those touched by its activities. The approach taken is typically driven by two things:

1 an organization's attitude and ambition towards sustainability (as discussed in the previous chapter);
2 the perceived risk to an organization's reputation if bad practice is exposed (this is discussed in Chapter 6).

Example – London Olympic and Paralympic Games 2012

The London Olympic and Paralympic Games 2012 bid was won on the ambition to host the most sustainable Games ever. Its vision is 'to use the power of the Games to inspire change'. Whether as athletes, spectators or simply supporters, everyone involved in the Games will help to change:

- people's lives;
- levels of sport and participation;
- attitudes to disability;
- the communities across London, particularly east London;
- sustainability and protecting the world we live in;
- how everyone participates in and engages with the Games;
- how cities host the Olympic and Paralympic Games.

Its sustainability policy sets out five priority themes:

Climate change   Waste   Biodiversity   Inclusion   Healthy living

Inclusion is discussed below. The intended social benefits of the priorities and commitments identified here cannot be delivered without aligned, sustainable supply chain practices.

Inclusion – the vision:

'To host the most inclusive Games to date by promoting access, celebrating diversity and facilitating the physical, economic and social regeneration of the Lower Lea Valley and surrounding communities.'

Inclusion priorities (that are relevant to its supply chain activities) have been identified as:

✓ ensuring that the opportunities provided by the Games are spread as widely and as fairly as possible;
✓ promoting supplier diversity and maximizing opportunities for local and UK minority-owned businesses and social enterprises to benefit;
✓ recruiting and developing a diverse workforce and ensuring opportunity and training are available to all;
✓ inspiring, engaging and involving people and communities across the UK in preparations for the Games and communities around the Olympic Park in developing legacy plans;
✓ creating excellent architecture and urban design, based on inclusive design principles, in the Olympic Park;
✓ achieving an equalities step-change in construction sector employment;
✓ using the Olympic Park Legacy to create sustainable, prosperous and cohesive new communities, fully integrated into the surrounding areas.

London 2012 also made the following commitments within its inclusion programme:

✓ London Employment and Skills Taskforce (LEST) to reduce worklessness in London by 70,000 by 2012;
✓ CompeteFor programme* to capture 20% of the estimated 75,000 total contract opportunities from the London 2012 supply chain;
✓ to provide 20,000 training places at the Olympic Park over five years from 2010 onwards.

*CompeteFor is an electronic brokerage service matching buyers and suppliers for the business opportunities related to the Olympic and Paralympic Games.

Case study source: London 2012 Sustainability Plan December 2009[10]

Supplier diversity

The importance of supplier diversity is rising up the sustainable procurement agenda across the UK and Europe with an increasing recognition that large organizations can benefit from a more diverse supply base. According to the *Handbook on Supplier Diversity in Europe* small businesses are underrepresented as first-tier suppliers, yet they contribute to 99.5 per cent of European businesses, employing more people than large companies and generating 37 per cent of private sector turnover in the UK.[11]

The *Handbook* considers supplier diversity to be 'the pro-active activity undertaken by large purchasing organizations to ensure that all relevant potential suppliers have the fair and equal opportunity to compete for business within their supply chains. This can include small businesses (i.e. those with fewer than 50 employees), medium-sized businesses (those with 50–249 employees), 'local' businesses and 'under-represented' businesses (small and medium firms and social enterprises that are minority owned and controlled by minority groups, including, but not limited to ethnic minorities, immigrants, women, disabled, lesbian, gay, bisexual and transgender people).'[11]

There are a number of different reasons for increasing the diversity of the supply base for larger organizations.

First, large organizations must respond to their external environment, they must offer products and services that are appropriate to an increasingly diverse marketplace. Finding and using a diverse supply base can help maintain this strategic alignment. Such suppliers can bring valuable insight, market knowledge and expertise.

> Procurement teams in the UK could be doing more to support minority suppliers. It's the start of a long journey. Buyers need to be educated on what these suppliers bring to the table.
>
> Mayank Shah, director, Minority Supplier Development UK[12]

Supplier diversity can also help build stakeholder relations and generate goodwill. Certain consumer groups may be more willing to buy from organizations that proactively include diverse suppliers, i.e. from suppliers owned by people like them.

Supplier diversity can also help an organization to achieve certain strategic objectives, playing a key role in demonstrating equality and inclusion and helping to contribute to a positive corporate image as a socially responsible organization.

Supplier diversity can also contribute to improved organizational performance as a wider pool of suppliers can generate competition, reduce cost and spread risk. Smaller and diverse suppliers often bring innovation and can be responsive and flexible when responding to customer requirements.

> A mass of evidence indicates that, at present, many small and medium sized businesses simply do not have access to information about what procurement opportunities are offered by large purchasing organizations.
>
> *Handbook on Supplier Diversity in Europe*, p.11

Often smaller organizations cannot compete for contracts simply due to the barriers put up during the procurement process. These include cumbersome and expensive pre-qualification procedures or consolidated, large contracts without the option to bid for smaller 'work packets'. We must recognize, however, that dividing larger contracts up into smaller work packets may not suit certain businesses and in these cases smaller businesses should be encouraged to compete lower down the supply chain. 'Meet the Buyer' events and systems like CompeteFor are ideal for this.

Current larger organizations take three approaches to tackle supplier diversity. These are:

1. 'Levelling the playing field' so that any company that wants to compete for a contract can do so. This is not showing a preference for smaller suppliers but just ensuring that they are able to compete equally for potential contracts.
2. 'Positive action' which targets suppliers in certain key groups and provides them with the opportunity to compete for contracts.
3. 'Requiring' suppliers to have diversity plans. Transport for London East London Line is a good example.[13] Also, London Organizing Committee of the Olympic Games (LOCOG) requires all suppliers to participate in the Diversity Works for London Scheme which is a ground-breaking campaign to encourage organizations to harness the benefits of a diverse workforce and supply base (see www.diversityworksforlondon.com/ for more information).

Sometimes the greatest challenges to achieving a more diverse supply base can be a resistance to change from internal stakeholders; procurement definitely has a role to play in enabling SMEs to reach a position where they have the necessary systems and processes required to become viable alternatives to larger organizations.

The Equality Act 2010 should also be mentioned here. This Act sets out new laws which aim to protect individuals from unfair treatment, creating a fairer and more equal society across the UK. It also strengthens and simplifies the law to make it easier for individuals and employers to understand their legal rights and obligations. At the time of writing, the government is considering how the different provisions will be commenced so that the Act is implemented in an effective and proportionate way. It is anticipated that this legislation could place specific requirements for public bodies to promote equalities and diversity through their procurement. (Public bodies spend over £220 billion a year, giving them a lot of buying power which can be used to encourage suppliers to treat people fairly in the way they do their work.) However, it is still unclear what the impact of this legislation on businesses could potentially be and the extent to which businesses will need to move away from a passive 'equal opportunities' approach to a more proactive strategy for equality.

The economic context

Economic considerations are the traditional heartland of decision making for procurement and sustainable procurement continues to recognize the fundamental importance of sound economic strategy. After all, a truly sustainable organization must be socially and environmentally responsible and economically viable over the long term.

From an economic perspective sustainable procurement encourages the use of more resource-efficient goods and services and encourages purchasers to evaluate cost performance over the lifetime of a contract and not limit decision making to upfront cost considerations. Whole-life costing (WLC) is increasingly being used. However, gaining comprehensive costing information and inflexible budgeting practices that do not allow for higher initial investments (with an inability to transfer funds between capital and operational budgets) can make decision making based on WLC principles particularly difficult. This subject will be discussed in detail in Chapter 7.

The economic pillar of sustainability also includes the need to drive job creation, develop new markets and foster innovation, such as in emerging green technologies or by creating markets for recycled products. For example, the previous Labour government predicted that the transition to a low-carbon economy will create approximately 400,000 jobs in the low-carbon environmental goods and services (LCEGS) sector by 2015.[14]

The creation of sustainable markets is essential for long-term growth. Additionally, ethical and responsible supply chain practices that ensure fair wages, working conditions and contract terms all go a long way towards providing a better quality of life for those employed in those supply chains. These issues also clearly demonstrate the interrelationship across the three pillars; green technologies, for example, generate economic benefits (including job creation, wealth generation, economic redistribution), social benefits (such as employment, training and skills development, supplier diversity) and environmental benefits (through more efficient use of resources).

The following example demonstrates how one company has boosted economic development across its supply chain by changing its buying practices and increasing the number of smaller suppliers.

Example – Economic development in the supply chain

Global brewer SABMiller is increasing the number of small farms it buys from to more than 30,000 by 2012 in parts of India, Latin America and Africa. The company estimates it has around 16,829 smallholder farmers who maintain around 10 hectares or less in 2009 and wants to increase this by more than 15,000 by 2012.

Encouraging sustainable development across its supply chain has been a key priority for the brewer which estimates for every person it employs it creates 40 jobs further down the supply chain. The firm indicates that local sourcing offers improved quality, more security of supply and savings through reducing the firm's reliance on imported raw materials.

Graham Mackay, CEO of SABMiller, said in a statement: 'A healthy growing environment in the communities where we operate is the key to business success'.

Source: *Supply Management*, 22 January 2009[15]

Sustainable development and virtuous cycles

Many of the issues and potential benefits surrounding sustainable business practices are interrelated; positive actions can frequently achieve social, environmental and economic benefits. Sometimes these positive actions have additional knock-on effects, which create further positive reinforcement that can result in benefits that go beyond initial expectations. The National Sailing Academy (while not supply chain focused) is an example of this positive spiral or 'virtuous cycle' concept of social, economic and environmental sustainability working in harmony. It also shows how social entrepreneurialism and public and private investment have come together to support a community with due respect to the environment.

Weymouth and Portland National Sailing Academy – a sustainability success story

Weymouth and Portland National Sailing Academy has become a world-class sailing facility. Its location, using the natural sweep of Portland Bay surrounded by World Heritage Jurassic coastline, forms a perfect competition space and natural amphitheatre. From a sustainability point of view, the venue has a great story to tell. According to CEO John Tweed, it started in 2003 with a couple of people with 'a vision and no money'.[16] The withdrawal of the MOD from Portland left this enchanting area of coastland with significant unemployment and economic problems long before the credit crunch. An area of contaminated land with some buildings, redundant fuel tanks and a slipway only suitable for hovercraft was acquired from the MOD by a new social enterprise to form the National Sailing Academy. A lot of hard work supported by investment from the National Lottery, the local Regional Development Agency and other donations saw the birth of a new organization.

The selection of the venue for the Olympics provided a further boost to the area and more investment by the Olympic Delivery Authority (ODA) to upgrade the facilities to Olympic standard. This involved additional hard-standing for boats, facilities for disabled sailors and improved slipway conditions. It is the first project ever to be awarded the highest CEEQUAL award for environmental excellence in civil engineering. The project had significant environmental challenges, from protection of coral, to habitats for seahorses and a rare microscopic worm that is unique to this particular bay.

The venue has become a social and economic success story. Elite sailors sail in the same water as children from local schools or families enjoying

---

introductory sailing courses. It aims to promote sailing at all levels and develop sailing as an 'inclusive sport'. The arrival of the Olympics has attracted private developers to build a marina that will be used during the Games but will also attract boat owners. As a result of this, an excellent restaurant has been opened nearby with more leisure and shopping facilities to come.

This brings much needed employment and economic regeneration to the area and studies by Dorset County Council estimate that the centre has created demand in service and marine industries worth in the region of £10 million. When all facilities are complete it is expected to add something in the region of £6 million each year to the local economy.[17]

Learning summary

This chapter has explored what sustainable procurement is and the principles associated with sustainable procurement. Sustainable procurement should not be seen as different or separate to the traditional process of procurement; it is a fundamental part of the procurement process. Sustainable procurement merely considers additional factors and attempts to maximize social, environmental and economic benefits for the organization, its supply chains and wider society. This means purchasers need to look beyond the conventional criteria of price, quality and service when making purchasing decisions with a view to maximizing benefits for themselves and the wider world. The beneficial outcomes that can be achieved by taking a more sustainable procurement approach are many and varied and will emerge over different timescales. For example, lower disposal costs of a product at the end of life (e.g. if the product can be recycled) may not be evident in the short term; alternatively, immediate economic benefits may be enjoyed by reducing consumption in the first place.

The key sustainability issues identified within the three pillars are diverse and many are interrelated. There are numerous examples of actions primarily taken to address one issue, having an influence on other sustainability themes. For example, the purchase of more energy-efficient goods not only reduces carbon emissions but has an economic benefit in terms of lower energy costs and also supports the drive towards greener products and green technologies. The example of Weymouth and Portland National Sailing Academy shows how sustainability themes are interrelated and that positive intervention can lead to significant benefits across many sustainability themes that go potentially beyond initial expectations.

Useful resources

BS 8900:2006, *Guidance for Managing Sustainable Development*, British Standards Institution, see: http://shop.bsigroup.com

Green Public Procurement (GPP), see: http://ec.europa.eu/environment/gpp/index_en.htm

Supplier Diversity Handbook, see: www.supplierdiversityeurope.eu

Diversity Works for London Toolkit, see: www.diversityworksforlondon.com

London 2012 Sustainability Plan December 2009 'Towards a One Planet 2012', see: www.london2012.com/documents/locog-publications/london-2012-sustainability-plan.pdf

Portal for Responsible Supply Chain Management. Access to tools and information to develop corporate social responsibility in the supply chain. See www.csr-supplychain.org

Action Sustainability Resources web pages. See www.actionsustainability.com/resources

'The UK Low Carbon Industrial Strategy'. See: www.berr.gov.uk/files/file52002.pdf

---

References

1 Supply Management 100 Poll November 2006, see: www.supplymanagement.com/analysis/features/2006/struggle-with-sustainability/
2 Supply Management 100 Poll November 2007, see: www.supplymanagement.com/news/2007/sustainable-buying-now-clearer/?locale=en
3 Sustainable Procurement Task Force, *Procuring the Future*, see www.defra.gov.uk/sustainable/government/documents/full-document.pdf
4 BS 8900:2006, *Guidance for managing sustainable development*, British Standards Institution.

---

5   NHS Carbon Reduction Strategy for England – NHS Carbon Footprint. NHS Sustainable Development Unit 2008. Retrieved from: www.sdu.nhs.uk/publications-resources/26/NHS-Carbon-Footprint/

6   'Some Companies Really do Make Greener Electronics', Greenpeace, 7 January 2010, see www.greenpeace.org/international/en/news/features/ces2010-some-companies-really-060110 and www.greenpeace.org/international/campaigns/toxics/electronics/how-the-companies-line-up)

7   Green v's sustainable Public Procurement. EUROPA. Retrieved from: http://ec.europa.eu/environment/gpp/versus_en.htm

8   'Clean Economy, Living Planet: Building Strong Clean Energy Technology Industries'. Retrieved from: http://assets.panda.org/downloads/rapport_wwf_cleaneconomy_international_def.pdf

9   London Leaders Brochure 2008: 'A Greater London What Are You Doing? Quotation Monica Saini, p.16; see: www.londonsdc.org/documents/What_are_you_doing_scn_12Oct07

10 London 2012 Sustainability Plan December 2009 'Towards a One Planet 2012', see: www.london2012.com/documents/locog-publications/london-2012-sustainability-plan.pdf

11 *Handbook on Supplier Diversity in Europe*. November 2009, CREME, Migration Policy Group. Retrieved from: www.supplierdiversityeurope.eu/news_details.php?id=82

12 'Buyers Should follow US Lead on Supplier Diversity. Jake Kanter, *Supply Management*, 27 March 2008.

13 www.london.gov.uk/rp/resources/events/20081124/presentation-kp-balfour.pdf

14 Innovas (2009) 'Low Carbon and Environmental Goods and Services: An Industry Analysis'. Retrieved from: www.berr.gov.uk/files/file50253.pdf

15 'Brewer Grows List of Local Farm Suppliers', Paul Snell, *Supply Management*, 22 January 2009. Retrieved from: www.supplymanagement.com/news/2009/brewer-grows-list-of-local-farm-supplies/?locale=en

16 'Catch the Wind'. Shaun McCarthy's blog, 21 August 2009, Commission for a Sustainable London 2012. Retrieved from: www.cslondon.org/2009/08/catch-the-wind/

17 Weymouth and Portland National Sailing Academy website archive see: http://web.archive.org/web/20070301094300/www.wpnsa.org.uk/background.htm

4. Why practise sustainable procurement?

Introduction

This chapter examines why sustainable procurement is important and what the main business drivers are. It also examines the policy context of sustainable procurement, summarizing public sector ambitions, commitments and progress so far. The final section of the chapter will examine the Flexible Framework which is a tool to enable organizations to assess their progress of sustainable procurement against best practice. This emerged from the Sustainable Procurement Task Force recommendations in its report *Procuring the Future* (2006). The Flexible Framework has since been instrumental in helping organizations to get started and make sustainable procurement happen.

What are the business drivers?

Cost savings and value

In general, cost saving is the single common measure of purchasing performance and there is often a perception that sustainable or 'green' goods and services cost more. This perception is supported by the 100 buyers sampled in the Supply Management SM 100 poll in August 2009 where just under two-thirds of the buyers indicated that they had not yet achieved significant savings from sustainable procurement (see Figure 8).[1] The key message should be that *sustainable procurement and cost savings are compatible*. At the most basic level what is it about using less energy, consuming fewer resources and sending less waste to landfill that costs more money? One could argue that the survey above did not ask the right question in the first place. The proper question should have been, have you seen significant 'whole of life' cost savings from sustainable procurement?

There are instances where sustainable alternatives will cost more upfront, but they are often cheaper in the long term when life cycle costs are considered. Typically, initial costs can be recovered over the full life cycle when energy consumption, water use, reuse and recycling potential and waste disposal costs are considered. However, this remains an enduring issue for buyers; i.e. the initial price may be higher (although not necessarily true) and the buyer finds it difficult or impossible to draw funds from future years to cover initial outlay even though future costs may be lower. It's the conundrum of cash/capital today versus future revenue.

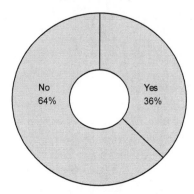

Figure 8 – SM 100 Poll: Have you achieved significant savings from implementing sustainable procurement?

A superb example of using life cycle costing to justify more sustainable solutions is the Durakerb recycled kerb solution that was sourced by Wakefield Metropolitan Council. The purchase price of these kerbstones (made from recycled plastic bottles) was over three times more expensive than traditional pre-cast kerb stones. However, when transport, installation, storage, maintenance and disposal costs were taken into account, the Durakerb solution became more cost-effective, offering better value for money over the expected life of the product.[2] It also provided additional environmental benefits including a reduction in CO_2 emissions and waste to landfill. Social benefits associated with the lightweight design meant a reduction in musculoskeletal injury risk for construction workers and further economic benefits were provided as faster installation meant reduced road closures and restrictions to the public.

Sustainability can create value and savings in other ways. One example taken from the construction sector was the decision by one constructor to increase wage levels to the recommended minimum levels such as the London Living Wage. Over the term of the contract this has had the effect of reducing staff turnover and increasing productivity.

Philip Dews, contract manager at facilities management firm Interserve sums the issue up realistically: 'Sustainable procurement is not a magic way to save money. It is about procuring goods in the right way, looking at the key aspects – social, economic and environmental. Cost is no longer the only consideration in procurement and sustainability has driven a more rounded approach that gives true value'. Buyers must also understand that suppliers will use the opportunity to treat sustainable products and services as a premium offering to increase their margins. It is the fundamental role of the buyer to challenge this and to use procurement professional skills to drive down cost *and* achieve sustainability.

There are also examples where sustainable procurement may cost more but in doing so it will right some fundamental wrongs and considerably reduce an organization's exposure to reputational damage. For example, instances where price competition is forcing suppliers into exploitative labour practices; a return to fair practice has the potential to drive up prices (this is discussed in more detail in Chapter 7).

The idea of delivering overall value across the lifetime of the goods, works or service lies at the heart of the sustainable procurement agenda, and the need for an organization to deliver social, economic and environmental value is being driven by many things, including legislation, stakeholder expectations, corporate image and risk, efficiency gains, competitive strategy and marketing. BS 8903, the British standard for sustainable procurement, sums this up using five main drivers (see Figure 9).

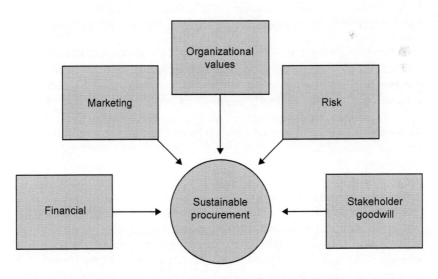

Figure 9 – Drivers of sustainable procurement

Why practise sustainable procurement?

Financial drivers include delivering operational cost savings over the contract life through:

✓ more efficient goods, works and services;
✓ challenging demand at source;
✓ reducing end-of-life disposal costs;
✓ driving efficiency in the supply chain.

Financial gains can also be made by developing market capacity for sustainable goods, works and services or by delivering innovative sustainable solutions that can enhance market share and competitiveness.

The long-term health of the supply chain to maintain both fair competition and security of supply is another reason for practising sustainable procurement. The MOD, for example, has formed an alliance (Aircraft Carrier Alliance) with BAE Systems Surface Ships, Babcock and Thales UK, and has awarded £333 million of contracts to companies across the UK to help to build the Royal Navy's new Queen Elizabeth Class aircraft carriers. This alliance harnesses skills, knowledge and manufacturing capacity from throughout the UK, spreading the workload, risks and rewards throughout the country, providing jobs and preserving UK shipbuilding.[3]

Marketing is another key driver which, in its simplest form, is about procuring goods with enhanced environmental or social credentials to either:

✓ drive more sales, e.g. ethical/fairly traded goods which target niche markets that exist for certain products, such as coffee, tea and chocolate. Divine chocolate is an example of how sustainability forms an inherent part of its product offering; this Fairtrade company is 45 per cent owned by farmers in Africa. While Fairtrade ensures farmers receive a better deal for their cocoa and additional income to invest in their community, company ownership gives farmers a share of Divine's profits and a stronger voice in the cocoa industry; or
✓ derive some positive image for the organization, which can help to differentiate organizations and build competitive advantage. The need to attract and retain the best talent is another reason to promote sustainability across an organization; matching personal and organizational values can help to maintain morale and staff loyalty. For example, FMC Technologies designs, manufactures and services sophisticated systems and products such as subsea production and processing systems for the oil and gas industry and talent is a major driver of its sustainability programme.

We are market leaders providing safe and reliable subsea equipment to operate in the most difficult conditions around the world. We need talented people to help us do this. Today's young people expect their employers to take their corporate social responsibilities seriously and so do I. I am proud to see my team live up to this challenge through implementing the highest standards of sustainability with our operations, customers and supply chain.

David Currie, Managing Director, FMC Technologies Ltd

Organizational values: these are typically reflected by an organization's mission statement, policy commitments and strategic targets. This is an expression of the culture, values and business ethos by which an organization operates which must be supported by procurement and reflected in procurement policy, strategy objectives, business practice and decision making. 'Plan A' by Marks & Spencer is a good example of this. This plan outlines the organization's mission to become the world's most sustainable retailer by 2015 and outlines 180 sustainability commitments to support this aim. Plan A has become an integral part of the company culture and fundamentally shapes business practice and decision making at every level across its business.

Risk: organizations must ensure that they understand what their key business risks are and that they have processes and controls in place to address them. Good sustainable procurement considers risk and should ensure that supply chain risks around security of supply, price volatility, moral and ethical risks and financial liabilities (through non-compliance with relevant legislation, for example) are managed and addressed. Undertaking an assessment of the supply chain risks within all the business's main categories of spend is good practice and will help to identify any unsustainable supply chain practices which have the potential to severely damage an organization's reputation and possibly even affect its licence to operate.

Hardly a month goes by without news of yet another company being brought into disrepute by exposure of unethical practices in its supply chains. In 2009 labour standards in the supply chain of the value clothing retailer Primark were called into question by the *Observer* newspaper and the BBC which claimed to have found poor conditions for employees at the retailer's Manchester-based supplier TNS Knitwear. The supplier had allegedly breached UK employment and immigration law.[4] In response Primark has agreed a 'wide-ranging' ethical trade action plan following an inquiry commissioned by the Ethical Trading Initiative

(ETI). During the investigation, a panel of independent experts found that Primark had 'significantly ramped up' its ethical trade activities since the initial allegations were made. These include the recruitment of a director of ethical trade; appointing ethical trade staff in sourcing countries; developing new ethical trade policies and practices; and raising the awareness of staff and suppliers through training.[5]

Stakeholders: are also demanding that organizations consider the environmental and social aspects of business and to implement sustainable initiatives (see Figure 10). Awareness is growing and both internal employees and external stakeholders are driving the need for change. Organizations must foster stakeholder goodwill and proactively and effectively address expectations and concerns. This can bring many benefits such as enhanced brand reputation or opening lines of dialogue on other issues; for example, improved communication may lead to a better understanding of the market and the external perceptions of the company which can be used to inform future strategy. Demonstrating responsible behaviour can help to smooth relationships and can reduce the risk of objections and adverse publicity. It may also help organizations to gain access to resources, skills and knowledge from stakeholders which would otherwise not have been made available.

For example, Greenpeace maintained an international campaign (Kleercut) against Kimberly-Clark, the world's largest manufacturer of tissue products, for nearly five years in an attempt to improve its paper policy. This forced a more collaborative approach and in 2009 after months of negotiation the manufacturer released 'the strongest paper policy' of the world's top three tissue product manufacturers. This policy committed to all Boreal Forest fibre purchases being FSC (Forest Stewardship Council) certified and 40 per cent of its North American tissue fibre to be either recycled or FSC certified by the end of 2011. It has also set the overall goal of obtaining 100 per cent of the company's wood fibre for tissue products from environmentally responsible sources.[6] (Note Boreal Forest is ancient woodland home to such species as grizzly and black bears, woodland caribou, wolves, bald eagles, boreal owls and pine marten.)

Legislation also acts as an important driver. However, it tends to shape the business practices of companies who lag in the areas of sustainable development. Leading companies are typically ahead of any legislation.

The CRC Energy Efficiency Scheme (formerly known as the Carbon Reduction Commitment) launched in the UK in April 2010 is a good example. This

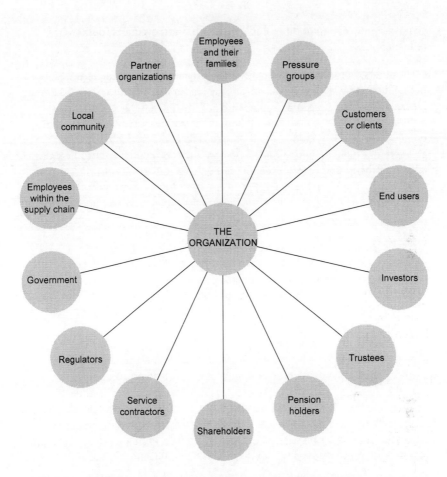

Figure 10 – An organization and its stakeholders

legislative driver is intended to force large organizations to adopt more energy-efficient practices and reduce carbon emissions. (It is compulsory for all non-energy intensive businesses and public sector organizations with an annual electricity spend of more than £500,000.) Companies must buy carbon allowances to cover their emissions which means firms must measure and record energy use and calculate their emissions (not including transport emissions). This is unlikely to change the energy policies of leading companies who proactively drive energy efficiency across their organizations and supply chains already. BT is a good example here; it has achieved a 58 per cent reduction in UK CO_2 emissions from a 1997 base.[7]

Many others, however, are not ready and have not made the necessary preparations to ensure compliance. Shortly before the launch of the CRC Energy Efficiency Scheme, Martin Rawlings, Chair of the CIPS Energy committee, estimated that 'at least one fifth of large organizations were nowhere near prepared for CRC legislation' and that many organizations were 'not even aware that it would apply to them'. He noted that even after four to five years in development, CRC communication and understanding was insufficient prior to its launch. This, combined with problems with the registration software prior to its launch, meant that many companies were ill prepared and unable to register in advance.

Marks & Spencer in the UK is one example of a leading company which remains ahead of legislative drivers. It has integrated sustainable development into its core business philosophy and has established demanding sustainable procurement policies to enhance its appeal to consumers and thus ultimately achieve competitive advantage. On the world stage, Wal-Mart has set up a sustainability index that grades suppliers and products by a range of environmental and sustainable factors. [8] This demand by Wal-Mart that its suppliers measure the environmental cost of making their products and ultimately give each item an eco-rating shows how leading companies are typically ahead of regulation. Interestingly, Wal-Mart, the world's largest retailer, doesn't differentiate on sustainability, it differentiates on price.[9] This suggests that stakeholder expectations are reaching new levels of maturity where responsible business practices are becoming a fundamental prerequisite and integrating sustainability should be considered 'business as usual'.

> The index will bring about a more transparent supply chain, drive product innovation and, ultimately, provide consumers [with] the information they need to assess the sustainability of products. If we work together, we can create a new retail standard for the twenty-first century.
>
> Mike Duke, President and Chief Executive Officer, Wal-Mart Stores, Inc. Walmart Sustainability Milestone Meeting, 16 July 2009

Sustainable procurement in the public sector – UK policy context

In 2005 the government published the Sustainable Development Strategy, *Securing the Future*, which set the target for the UK 'to be recognised as amongst the leaders in sustainable procurement across EU member states by 2009'.[10] As a result the government established the Sustainable Procurement Task Force under the leadership of Sir Neville Simms. The taskforce was charged with creating a National Action Plan to embed sustainability within UK public sector procurement. The Task Force published its recommendations in 2006 in *Procuring the Future*.[11] This report clarified what is meant by sustainable procurement and proposed a comprehensive set of measures to address shortcomings in public sector procurement. Six key recommendations were made:

1. The government must *lead by example*. Lack of consistent leadership was cited as a key barrier, with a need to demonstrate consistent commitment and direction from the top of public sector organizations.
2. The government must *set clear priorities* and rationalize the significant number of (sometimes competing) policies through procurement into a single integrated sustainable procurement framework.
3. The government must *raise the bar*, requiring that existing minimum standards for central government should be enforced and extended to the rest of the public sector. Further standards should be developed in the priority areas of: construction, energy, food, furniture, health and social work, office machinery, pulp and paper, textiles, transport and waste. The intention is to raise performance within buying and selling organizations and provide clear signals to the marketplace on future requirements.
4. The public sector must *build capacity* by developing capabilities to deliver sustainable procurement. It requested improvements in the quality of information, messages, training and tools for purchasers. A flexible framework has been developed to enable public sector organizations to benchmark their own capability.
5. The government must *remove barriers* to sustainable procurement, whether actual or perceived. These include budgetary constraints, the failure to implement whole-life costing, the split between management of operation and capital budgets, and uncertainty on how to take account of non-monetary benefits. HM Treasury is to simplify and clarify existing guidance on whole-life costing.
6. The public sector must *capture opportunities* for innovation and social benefits and better manage risk through smarter engagement with the market.

Why practise sustainable procurement?

The government responded to *Procuring the Future* with the publication of *Transforming Government Procurement*[12] and the UK Government Sustainable Procurement Action Plan[13] (SPAP) in 2007. These documents set out the actions to create a transformation in public services and government supply chains to be increasingly low carbon, low waste, water efficient, respect biodiversity and deliver wider sustainable development goals. It also set new Sustainable Operations on the Government Estate (SOGE) targets (see below). The cumulative effect of achieving these targets was estimated to deliver savings of approximately 1 million tonnes of carbon emissions by 2020.[14]

Sustainable Operations on the Government Estate (SOGE) targets:

- reduce carbon emissions from offices by 12.5 per cent by 2010–11, relative to their 1999–2000 levels;
- reduce carbon emissions from offices by 30 per cent by 2020, relative to their 1999–2000 levels;
- achieve carbon neutrality for the central government estate by 2012;
- departments to increase energy efficiency per m^2 by 15 per cent by 2010 and 30 per cent by 2020, relative to 1999–2000 levels; and
- these targets are in addition to pre-existing targets for departments to source at least 10 per cent electricity from renewables by April 2008 and 15 per cent from combined heat and power by 2010.

Source: DEFRA, see: www.defra.gov.uk/sustainable/government/gov/estates/targets.htm (Note these targets were published in 2006 and may alter with the change of government.)

The role of the Office of Government Commerce (OGC) was also revised. Initially, the OGC was tasked with working in partnership with all government departments to improve all aspects of procurement including sustainability. However, in response to the Task Force's criticisms over a lack of defined leadership and ownership of sustainability within public sector procurement, the OGC's remit extended to it becoming 'accountable for embedding agreed (sustainable) procurement policies'.[13]

In 2008 the Centre of Excellence for Sustainable Procurement (CESP) was also set up and is administered by the OGC (take care not to confuse CESP with the Community Energy Saving Programme). CESP is intended to provide stronger central co-ordination of performance and to raise capability and leadership in sustainable procurement. It is also intended to provide guidance and support to government departments, and to help those departments meet SOGE targets and SPAP commitments. It should also set out plans to help to counter barriers that stand in the way of government progress.

So what progress has been made? A 2009 National Audit Office report[15] concluded that 'government had strengthened its drive to purchase more environmentally sustainable goods and services'. However, a number of departments were 'not yet on course to be practising sustainable procurement across their businesses by the end of 2009', in line with government targets. Barbara Morton, co-author of the 2008 report 'Costing the Future', also stated that 'Many of the necessary policies and regulations have been put in to place, however they have not been translated into practice. Examples of best practice exist, but there is a plethora of missed opportunities'.[16]

> Many sustainable development practitioners will still see sustainable procurement as simply purchasing from lists of recommended goods and services.
>
> *Sustainable Development in Government*, Sustainable Development Commission, March 2008[16]

Value Wales, the procurement arm of the Welsh Assembly Government, in its 2009/2010 report *Adding Value II – Showcasing Examples of Good Practice in Procurement and Delivery* illustrates examples of how areas of the public sector are demonstrating leading practice. This report shows that public procurement is about much more than delivering lowest cost and demonstrates the potential to support wider well-being by encouraging greater sustainability or stimulating innovation and efficiency.[17]

In 2008/09 the public sector spent around £220 billion on the procurement of goods and services, and there is a growing recognition that this spend should be used to deliver wider policy objectives. These wider policy objectives include environmental issues, removing barriers to SME participation in public procurement, fostering innovation and promoting equality of opportunity. As a result, the 'Policy through Procurement' initiative was established and the OCG has developed an action plan which sets out how the government will deliver these policies.

The plan shows how procurement will be used to pursue economic growth through the three priority agendas of supporting SMEs; encouraging apprenticeships, training and youth employment; and reducing carbon emissions. (See www.ogc.gov.uk/ policy_and_standards_framework_policy_through_procurement.asp for more information.)

Further public policy initiatives that are picked up in the policy through procurement initiative include the recommendations made in the Glover Report (November 2008)[18] which examines what the government could do to make it easier for SMEs to supply to the public sector. Also 'New Industry, New Jobs',[19] BERR (now BIS), April 2009, outlines the aspiration for public procurement to have a role in shaping markets and using strategic procurement as a key to encouraging innovation and transforming the UK to a low-carbon economy.

Green Public Procurement, also known as GPP, is an EU initiative that must also be mentioned here. GPP means that public procurers across the EU member states take into account environmental factors when purchasing goods, works or services. It captures how environmental policy objectives can be promoted and delivered through procurement. (The EU GPP toolkit can be found at http://ec.europa.eu/environment/gpp/index_en.htm.)

The toolkit consists of three independent modules, each designed to overcome a specific problem identified as a barrier to the uptake of GPP. Across the UK, the political target for 2010 was that 50 per cent of all central government and wider government tenders should be compliant with the core GPP criteria by the end of that year.

Getting started with sustainable procurement: the Flexible Framework

The Task Force produced the Flexible Framework (see Table 3), which is a tool to help public sector organizations get started and make sustainable procurement happen. This framework was based on advice from a business-led taskforce and was based on experience of leading businesses at the time. It clarifies the steps needed at an organizational and process level to improve procurement practice and covers five themes:

1 people;
2 policy, strategy and communication;
3 procurement process;
4 engaging suppliers; and
5 measurement and results.

Table 3 – The Flexible Framework

	Foundation Level 1	Embed Level 2	Practice Level 3	Enhance Level 4	Lead Level 5
People	Sustainable procurement champion identified. Key procurement staff have received basic training in sustainable procurement principles. Sustainable procurement is included as part of a key employee induction programme.	All procurement staff have received basic training in sustainable procurement principles. Key staff have received advanced training on sustainable procurement principles.	Targeted refresher training on latest sustainable procurement principles. Performance objectives and appraisal include sustainable procurement factors. Simple incentive programme in place.	Sustainable procurement included in competencies and selection criteria. Sustainable procurement is included as part of employee induction programme.	Achievements are publicized and used to attract procurement professionals. Internal and external awards are received for achievements. Focus is on benefits achieved. Good practice shared with other organizations.
Policy, strategy and communications	Agree overarching sustainability objectives. Simple sustainable procurement policy in place endorsed by CEO. Communicate to staff and key suppliers.	Review and enhance sustainable procurement policy, in particular consider supplier engagement. Ensure it is part of a wider Sustainable Development strategy. Communicate to staff, suppliers and key stakeholders.	Augment the sustainable procurement policy into a strategy covering risk, process integration, marketing, supplier engagement, measurement and a review process. Strategy endorsed by CEO.	Review and enhance the sustainable procurement strategy, in particular recognizing the potential of new technologies. Try to link strategy to EMS and include in overall corporate strategy.	Strategy is: reviewed regularly, externally scrutinized and directly linked to organization's EMS. The Sustainable Procurement strategy, recognized by political leaders, is communicated widely. A detailed review is undertaken to determine future priorities and a new strategy is produced beyond this framework.

	Foundation Level 1	Embed Level 2	Practice Level 3	Enhance Level 4	Lead Level 5
Procurement process	Expenditure analysis undertaken and key sustainability impacts identified. Key contracts start to include general sustainability criteria. Contracts awarded on the basis of value-for-money, not lowest price. Procurers adopt Quick Wins.	Detailed expenditure analysis undertaken, key sustainability risks assessed and used for prioritization. Sustainability is considered at an early stage in the procurement process of most contracts. Whole-life cost analysis adopted.	All contracts are assessed for general sustainability risks and management actions identified. Risks managed throughout all stages of the procurement process. Targets to improve sustainability are agreed with key suppliers.	Detailed sustainability risks assessed for high-impact contracts. Project/contract sustainability governance is in place. A life cycle approach to cost/impact assessment is applied.	Life cycle analysis has been undertaken for key commodity areas. Sustainability Key Performance Indicators agreed with key suppliers. Progress is rewarded or penalized based on performance. Barriers to sustainable procurement have been removed. Best practice shared with other organizations.
Engaging suppliers	Key supplier spend analysis undertaken and high sustainability impact suppliers identified. Key suppliers targeted for engagement and views on procurement policy sought.	Detailed supplier spend analysis undertaken. General programme of supplier engagement initiated, with senior manager involvement.	Targeted supplier engagement programme in place, promoting continual sustainability improvement. Two-way communication between procurer and supplier exists with incentives. Supply chains for key spend areas have been mapped.	Key suppliers targeted for intensive development. Sustainability audits and supply chain improvement programmes in place. Achievements are formally recorded. CEO involved in the supplier engagement programme.	Suppliers recognized as essential to delivery of organization's sustainable procurement strategy. CEO engages with suppliers. Best practice shared with other/peer organizations. Suppliers recognize they must continually improve their sustainability profile to keep the client's business.

| Measurements and results | Key sustainability impacts of procurement activity have been identified. | Detailed appraisal of the sustainability impacts of the procurement activity has been undertaken. Measures implemented to manage the identified high-risk impact areas. | Sustainability measures refined from general departmental measures to include individual procurers and are linked to development objectives. | Measures are integrated into a balanced score card approach reflecting both input and output. Comparison is made with peer organizations. Benefit statements have been produced. | Measures used to drive organizational sustainable development strategy direction. Progress formally benchmarked with peer organizations. Benefits from sustainable procurement are clearly evidenced. Independent audit reports available in the public domain. |

© Crown Copyright 2006, *Procuring the Future*

The Flexible Framework forms the cornerstone of the Sustainable Procurement National Action Plan and the aim is to enable all organizations to find their place on it and then take actions to move through five levels (from 1– Foundation through to 5 – Lead) as sustainable procurement is implemented. The Task Force recommended that all public sector organizations should be level 3 by 2009 and at level 5 in at least one area. (Pan-government performance is measured and recorded; see the OGC website for summary of progress.)

The Flexible Framework was primarily intended as a guide to demonstrate how organizations can achieve better performance. It has evolved into a self-assessment tool and as such scoring can be inconsistent between organizations. It has been around for some time now and although it has been criticized for not measuring actual outcomes, it is still a useful tool which can also help private sector organizations identify steps to take to improve sustainable procurement practice. Action Sustainability provides an online Flexible Framework Evaluation Tool which helps organizations assess their practices (see useful resources section for web link).

Summary

This chapter has explored the business drivers of sustainable procurement. BS 8903 identifies five primary drivers including financial, marketing, risk, organizational values and stakeholder goodwill. Legislation is another key driver, but this tends to apply more to organizations that lag in terms of sustainable business practice. Leading organizations recognize the potential benefits to reputation, consumer appeal and to meet stakeholders' (including employees') increasing demands for responsible business practices. These companies are typically ahead of regulatory enforcement. The speed of change of the sustainable procurement agenda has been remarkable over the past few years, to the extent that in some sectors, addressing sustainability through the supply chain is not so much a source of competitive advantage but is rapidly becoming a source of competitive disadvantage.

The public sector has a key role to play in sustainable procurement and this spending power, if used effectively, can drive better business practices, shape new markets and stimulate innovation for more sustainable products and services. The Sustainable Procurement National Action Plan *Procuring the Future* (2006) was a very influential report and its findings have shaped public purchasing policy over the past four years. The Flexible Framework was a cornerstone of this report and remains a key tool to help both public and private sector organizations get started with sustainable procurement.

Useful resources

Durakerb Sustainable Procurement Case Study – retrieved from www.procurementcupboard.org

'Plan A', Marks & Spencer, see: http://plana.marksandspencer.com/we-are-doing

Sustainable Procurement Task Force, *Procuring the Future*, DEFRA, 2006. See: www.defra.gov.uk/sustainable/government/documents/full-document.pdf

Transforming Government Procurement, HM Treasury, January 2007. See: www.hm-treasury.gov.uk/d/government_procurement_pu147.pdf

'Costing the Future', Securing Value for Money through Sustainable Procurement. Westminster Sustainable Business Forum, June 2008.

OGC Policy through Procurement Initiative/Action Plan, see: www.ogc.gov.uk/policy_and_standards_framework_policy_through_procurement.asp

'Addressing the environmental impacts of Government procurement', NAO Report, 29 April 2009. See: www.nao.org.uk/publications/0809/addressing_sustainable_procure.aspx

Action Sustainability Flexible Framework Online Assessment Tool, see www.actionsustainability.com/evaluation/flexible_framework/

References

1   'Sustainable Procurement Is "Low Priority" for Purchasers', Allie Anderton, Supply Management Web news, 19 August 2009. Retrieved from: www.supplymanagement.com/news/2009/sustainable-procurement-is-low-priority-for-purchasers/?locale=en
2   Sustainable Procurement Case Study: Durakerb. Retrieved from www.procurementcupboard.org

3   The Aircraft Carrier Alliance. MOD news, 14 January 2010. Retrieved from:
    www.modoracle.com/news/The-Aircraft-Carrier-Alliance_19667.html
4   'Primark in Storm over Conditions at UK Supplier', Dan McDougall, *Observer*,
    11 January 2009. Retrieved from: www.guardian.co.uk/business/2009/jan/
    11/primark-ethical-business-living
5   'UK: Ethical trade action plan agreed for Primark', Juststyle.com,
    21 January 2010. Retrieved from: www.just-style.com/news/
    ethical-trade-action-plan-agreed-for-primark_id106485.aspx
6   'Kimberly-Clark and Greenpeace agree to historic measures to protect
    forests'. Retrieved from: www.kleercut.net/en
7   'Changing the World: Sustained Values – Our 2009 Sustainability Review'.
    BT Group plc, sustainability review 2009.
8   'Walmart taps CDP for Emissions Reporting in Sustainability Index'. *Environmental
    Leader*, 16 July 2009. Retrieved from: www.environmentalleader.com/
    2009/07/16/wal-mart-tabs-cdp-for-emissions-reporting-in-sustainability-index
9   'Climate of Change', *Supply Management*, Andy Allen, 7 January 2010.
    Retrieved from www.supplymanagement.com/analysis/features/2010/
    climate-of-change
10 *Securing the Future*, 1995. Retrieved from: www.defra.gov.uk/sustainable/
    government/publications/uk-strategy
11 Sustainable Procurement Task Force, *Procuring the Future*, DEFRA, 2006.
    Retrieved from www.defra.gov.uk/sustainable/government/documents/
    full-document.pdf
12 *Transforming Government Procurement*, HM Treasury, January 2007. Retrieved
    from: www.hm-treasury.gov.uk/d/government_procurement_pu147.pdf
13 Sustainable Procurement Action Plan, March 2007. Retrieved from:
    www.defra.gov.uk/sustainable/government/documents/
    SustainableProcurementActionPlan.pdf
14 'Costing the Future', Securing Value for Money through Sustainable
    Procurement. Westminster Sustainable Business Forum, June 2008, p.12.
15 'Addressing the environmental impacts of Government procurement'.
    NAO Report, 29 April 2009. Retrieved from: www.nao.org.uk/publications/0809/
    addressing_sustainable_procure.aspx
16 'Costing the Future', June 2008.
17 *Adding Value II – Showcasing Examples of Good Practice in Procurement
    and Delivery*. Value Wales. Retrieved from: http://wales.gov.uk/docs/dpsp/
    publications/valuewales/100720addingvalue0910env1.pdf

18 *Accelerating the SME Economic Engine: Through Transparent, Simple and Strategic Procurement.* November 2008 (also known as the Glover Report). Retrieved from: www.hm-treasury.gov.uk/glover_review_index.htm

19 'New Industry, New Jobs', BERR (now BIS), April 2009. Retrieved from: www.bis.gov.uk/policies/new-industry-new-jobs

5. BS 8903: An overview

Introduction

This chapter examines and summarizes BS 8903 *Principles and framework for procuring sustainably*. This standard is a guidance standard only. This means it is a generic guide which does not 'specify' exactly the steps that must be taken to ensure sustainable procurement, rather it provides insight, information and recommendations regarding sustainable procurement practice. It is split into three sections:

1   What is sustainable procurement?
2   Why procure sustainably?
3   How to do sustainable procurement.

> The first two sections have been discussed in Chapters 3 and 4 of this book, so this chapter will summarize the third section, which forms the largest section of the standard. Figure 11 provides an overview of its key themes.

These themes are further grouped into:

> Fundamentals – these are the higher-level organizational and procurement policies and strategies that should be in place to provide the strategic context and identify the strategic priorities. These should guide decision making and sustainable procurement practice.
> Procurement process – BS 8903 follows a generic procurement process and identifies the sustainability considerations and activities that should be addressed at various points across this process.
> Enablers – these include ways of working, competencies, practices and techniques that should be in place and utilized by managers or buyers on an ongoing or periodic basis. These enablers *support* the activities within the procurement process.

Fundamentals – the starting point

The first step is to establish what sustainability means for your organization and what the key priorities are. Procurement objectives must be aligned with the business priorities of the organization, creating a clear link back to the core

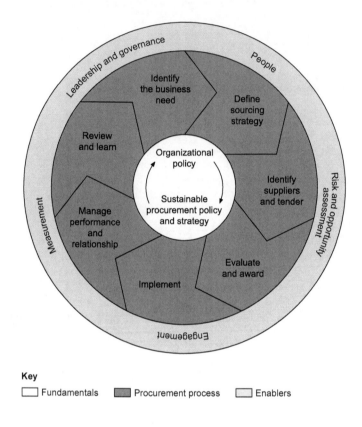

Key

☐ Fundamentals ▨ Procurement process ☐ Enablers

Figure 11 – BS 8903 Sustainable procurement overview

purpose of the business. As such, organizational sustainability policy (and/or strategy) should be the starting point for any sustainable procurement programme.

Organizational policy

Organizations typically have a clear, written statement as to the company values, mission and strategic goals. This statement may be called a strategy or a policy (or other) but should clearly state what sustainability means to that organization and what its intentions and objectives are. In some cases organizations have a single policy statement which includes its sustainability aims, in others this may still be written as a separate document. Either way this reflects the ethos, culture and values of the organization and should demonstrate the alignment of any sustainability objectives with the business priorities.

This statement is the starting point of any sustainable procurement activity as it provides the foundation, strategic direction and priorities relevant to that organization. This should ensure that procurement is aligned with the organizational goals and sustainable development aspirations of the business. If this can be done, senior management support (which is essential), is much easier to obtain.

However, this shouldn't be considered just a 'top-down process', and in some cases procurement may influence that policy, for example, significant developments in the supply chain or market research completed by purchasing may result in a revision to organizational goals and sustainability intentions. This was the case for United Utilities (UU), a UK plc based in north-west England, providing water and wastewater services throughout the north-west. In 2008 it embarked on a comprehensive development of sustainable procurement and found that the Supply Chain team had sustainability ambitions beyond the current organization's stated aims. With strong procurement leadership, a new corporate responsibility policy was produced to reflect this new ambition which included helping improve the sustainability performance of the entire supply chain.

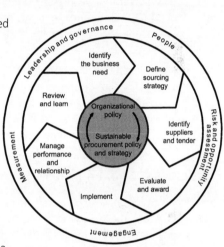

The supply chain department has since aligned supplier measures with the company measures. By doing this it is possible to have clarity of purpose from the boardroom right down to the supplier at the lowest tier of the supply chain. The role of the supply chain professional is to prioritize these business objectives through the supply chain and translate them into contractual arrangements and supplier performance outcomes.

Sustainability goals and aspirations will differ between organizations and projects: this means what may be at the top of one organization's priority list may not be a significant issue for another organization. For example, London 2012 has identified five priority sustainability themes (climate change, waste, inclusion, biodiversity and healthy living), Transport for London's (TFL's) sustainable development agenda includes developing responsible procurement, increasing accessibility of public transport, cycling and walking across London, climate change, sustainable road freight and building a sustainable transport network as its key priorities. Willmott Dixon, a major construction contractor, in 2009 focused delivery of its sustainable development agenda using four headline themes: putting people first, climate change and energy efficiency, smarter use of natural resources and responsible business.

For more information see:

- London 2012 sustainability policy: www.london2012.com/documents/locog-publications/london-2012-sustainability-policy.pdf
- Sustainable development at TFL: www.tfl.gov.uk/corporate/about-tfl/8127.aspx
- Willmott Dixon, Sustainable Development Review: http://sdreview2009.re-thinkingcommunications.com

Procurement policy and strategy

Some organizations have separate sustainable procurement policy and strategy statements, others may merge these into a single document. The key point is that a clearly written statement(s) outlining the main sustainability intentions and priorities for procurement is needed. Buyers have to manage diverse criteria and challenges when developing and managing supply chains and they need to understand what the main sustainability goals are. This can be achieved by providing clear, consistent guidance on the high-level priorities which should then assist decision making and ensure alignment. Often as experience of sustainability grows, the sustainable procurement policy and/or strategy merges with the overall procurement strategy in line with the principle that sustainable procurement is good, basic procurement practice.

In summary, a good sustainable procurement policy and strategy should:

✓ be aligned with the organizational drivers for sustainable development;
✓ be informed by an initial high-level sustainable procurement risk and opportunity assessment. This is needed to identify and prioritize the appropriate issues and opportunities relevant to your business;

✓ capture all three pillars of sustainability, i.e. the economic, social and environmental considerations;

✓ identify the key sustainable procurement targets, objectives and measures (key performance indicators);

✓ be endorsed or led by senior management; and

✓ be communicated to all staff, key suppliers and other key stakeholders at the most appropriate time.

There are many examples of good sustainable procurement strategy, such as the construction organization Willmott Dixon (WD). It aims to take a leadership role in sustainability in the built environment and in 2009 received third place in the Sunday Times Best Green Companies award. WD launched a Sustainable Supply Chain Strategy in 2009 intended to:

• provide leadership within the industry;
• ensure suppliers are aware of WD's sustainability objectives;
• enhance compliance with WD's sustainability objectives;
• bring best value to all parties concerned;
• help suppliers to become more sustainable;
• identify key risks in different trade sectors;
• provide year-on-year improvement;
• minimize damage to, and enhance, the environment;
• retain and satisfy WD's current clients;
• assist WD in winning more competitive business, from high-quality clients that share the same commitment to the sustainable development agenda;
• drive innovation and share best practice; and
• be ahead of competitors in the market.

For a copy of WD's sustainable supply chain strategy, see: www.willmottdixongroup.co.uk/careers/our-values-and-culture/corporate-responsibility

Risk

Note that an understanding of the key sustainability risks and opportunities affecting the organization, its supply chain and sector is fundamental to identifying appropriate strategic objectives and enabling priorities and key performance indicators to be agreed. This is returned to in the next chapter.

Procurement process

BS 8903 examines a generic
procurement process from end to
end, starting with identification
of the business need through
to supplier performance
management and final review
at the end of the contract life.
It discusses the sustainable
procurement considerations
that emerge across this process.
It does *not* detail the public sector
procurement rules and the impact
this has on sustainable procurement.

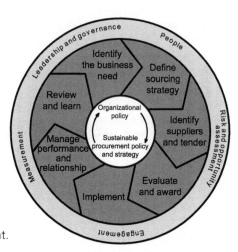

Unlike the standard, this chapter will only summarize the sustainability considerations
and potential tools and techniques that may be useful at each process stage. It
provides only a brief overview of each stage including some relevant examples.

1 Identify business need

Most purchases begin with the identification of a
need, which usually results from either:

- a new requirement for goods, works
  or service;
- resolution to a business issue or
  business risk, for example, a security
  of supply risk or changes in
  regulatory requirements;
- pursuit of strategy objectives, for
  example, meeting cost savings, supplier
  rationalization or carbon reduction targets.

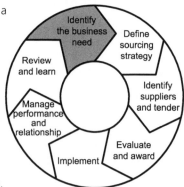

> To maximize opportunities for sustainability, it should be considered at the
> very outset of the procurement process.
>
> 'Buying a Better World, Forum for the Future', December 2007

The best time to deliver sustainable procurement is at the start of the process. Failure to do this will result in lost opportunity because a buyer or designer's ability to influence cost, performance and sustainability declines as the procurement process progresses. Also, the most fundamental sustainable challenge comes at this point, that is, to question the actual need in the first place. Remember, the most sustainable product that you buy is the one that you don't buy at all.

The key activity at this stage is to understand the current and future needs of the key stakeholders. Buyers should not simply request a specification but should attempt to understand and challenge the business requirements and try to distinguish between stakeholder wants and needs. This will help to identify all potential strategy options and selection of the best possible procurement solution. Defining the need or business requirement is not necessarily simple – it can have a major impact on the final specification and is a significant point of intervention to influence sustainability.

Business requirements typically include regulatory requirements, quality and performance requirements, service, cost, innovation and supply requirements. Sustainability requirements should also be factored in here and should be aligned with the organizational sustainability objectives. For example, if an organizational strategy is to reduce energy consumption, then any potential solutions should also strive to achieve this aim.

Buyers should challenge and question repeat purchases and seek innovative ways to meet business requirements. Attempt to change mindsets to move away from tight product specifications to output/outcome-based ones (i.e. shift from products to services and performance-based requirements; this means identifying the desired outcomes and letting the suppliers decide how best to meet your needs).

Key points

1. *The procurement requirement should always be framed within the parameters set by the organization's policies.*
2. *Accurately defining the need or business requirement is not always simple but is important because:*
   a. *it has a major impact on the final specification;*
   b. *it is a significant point of intervention to influence sustainability outcomes; and*
   c. *it can give suppliers flexibility to innovate and identify sustainable solutions.*

2 Define sourcing strategy

Depending on the size and scale of the purchase, further market research may be required before all the purchasing options can be defined. If there are a number of possible purchasing solutions under consideration, some formal evaluation of these options will also be required. From a sustainability perspective market research should be encouraged to promote creativity and determine if new technologies, new products, new innovative suppliers or advances in sustainable business practices could meet business requirements. *Innovation is critical to making real advances in delivering sustainable solutions.* There are many examples of how companies are attempting to achieve this, such as:

℘ Unilever, owner of Ben and Jerry's ice cream, has launched a room-temperature ice-cream project. The company is attempting to develop an ice cream that consumers can buy at room temperature, thereby removing the need for refrigerated transport and storage. Consumers would need to freeze the product at home, but the overall energy used would be reduced.[1]

℘ In 2010 BAA started operating driverless cars at Heathrow, carrying passengers from car parks to Terminal 5.[2]

℘ London 2012 will purchase enough tensile plastic to wrap around Canary Wharf Tower twice. By using its purchasing leverage the ODA issued a 10-point specification for the material, two of which could not be met at the time. As a result of this, an Italian manufacturer has developed a product free of carcinogenic chemicals and made the world a safer place.

℘ In 2010, constructor Bovis Lend Lease committed to use an innovative 5-litre fuel can that regulates the flow of fuel allowing users to estimate the amount delivered and reduce wastage. The can does not give off air emissions and cannot spill. This procurement commitment will enable the supplying company (which employs seven people on the Isle of Wight) to develop a new 20-litre version that will better support Bovis's operation and enable more people to be employed in an area of high unemployment.

Buyers need to think beyond their ownership and use of a product and consider all stages of production, transportation, use and disposal as sustainability impacts are created throughout the whole product life cycle.

Where sustainability requirements cannot be met in the current market, forward commitment procurement (FCP) may also be used by buyers to encourage potential suppliers to innovate and create new sustainable solutions. This is a demand–pull process that begins from the identification of an unmet need. This is a need that current products and services available in the market cannot deliver or can only do so at excessive cost or with unacceptable risk.

In brief, FCP involves providing the market with information of unmet needs and the incentive of a forward commitment, i.e. an agreement to purchase a product or service that currently might not exist, at a specified date in the future, providing it can be delivered to agreed performance levels and cost. This is discussed in more detail in Chapter 8.

All possibilities (including FCP opportunities) should be evaluated before any decisions are made on the final purchasing solution and resulting specification. There are a number of sustainability tools and techniques that can be used to help buyers and project teams decide this. These include:

Life cycle assessment (LCA) – This is the compilation and evaluation of inputs, outputs and the potential environmental impacts of a product system throughout its life cycle. In the context of LCA, an environmentally preferable product is a product that has the minimum environmental impacts throughout its life cycle, compared with other products or services of the same function and purpose. (See useful resources section to reference more LCA information.)

Carbon measurement – This follows the LCA approach but is focused on measuring the carbon footprint of products across their full life cycle. It analyses carbon emissions across the complete supply chain from raw material to end consumer. (See useful resources section to reference more carbon measurement information.)

Whole-life costing (WLC) – This involves estimating the costs of a product or service over its lifetime; this includes purchase, set-up, maintenance, operating and disposal costs. It involves identifying future costs and referring them back to the present-day costs using standard accounting techniques such as net present value. WLC is discussed in more detail in Chapter 7. WLC is also frequently used at the tender evaluation stage to ensure cost evaluation is not based on purchase price alone.

Risk and opportunity analysis – Buyers should review the risks and opportunities of any potential purchasing options against the organization's sustainability objectives. This will ensure buyers can prioritize the highest-impact aspects and identify appropriate interventions, mitigating measures and qualification criteria throughout the pre-qualification or tender process. Risk assessment is covered in more detail in Chapter 6.

Weighted decision making – This is a structured decision-making process and involves evaluating the purchasing options against a defined set of requirements. These requirements should be aligned with business objectives and incorporate key sustainability impacts and opportunities. They should also capture the relevant commercial and functional requirements. Agreeing and allocating relevant weighting ensures that appropriate consideration is given to each requirement and that sustainable requirements are not ignored or underestimated. This process also enables buyers to balance WLC thinking alongside conclusions drawn from other analysis such as risk and impacts analysis or LCA.

Finalizing the specification
Once the purchasing option has been selected the specification can be finalized. The specification is the most effective means of ensuring sustainable aspects are incorporated into the purchasing decision. (Note that for public sector procurement, provided that all requirements are relevant to the subject matter, a buyer has significant freedom to design these in.) Specifications should be used to establish minimum acceptable performance, actively excluding undesirable features and specifying in positive aspects and preferred higher sustainability options. Table 4 outlines three typical approaches to designing in sustainability criteria, which are listed in the first column. It then illustrates how sustainability criteria can be incorporated into the specification using these differing approaches. (Note: it is important that the sustainability criteria should be aligned with the high-level organizational sustainability objectives such as climate change mitigation.)

Table 4 – Different specification approaches and example criteria

Specification approach	Examples of impact criteria linked to organization objectives		
	Climate change mitigation	Waste reduction	Social risk/benefit
Physical features	Energy efficiency standards for goods (e.g. Government Buying Standards, Energy Star, etc.)	Reusable or recyclable product	Product for disposal for some social gain (e.g. use by a charity)
Process	Standards for embedded energy impacts in manufacture or service provision/construc tion	Waste targets in manufacturing process or 'take-back' arrangement at end of life	Materials that are not harmful to health in manufacture (e.g. PVC) or from sources causing social damage (e.g. coltan)
Outcome/perfor mance	Energy targets for service contracts (e.g. facilities management)	Waste targets for projects (e.g. construction)	Labour requirements for services (e.g. apprenticeships)

Key points

1 *Look for innovative solutions to meet business needs in a more sustainable way.*
2 *Harness suppliers' expertise and research the market to understand what sustainable solutions may be available.*
3 *If sustainable solutions do not exist yet, take responsibility and signal to the market what your needs are, to encourage suppliers to respond and develop sustainable solutions.*
4 *Where possible, include sustainability requirements into your specification; this will ensure that sustainability requirements are included in decision making.*

3 Identify suppliers and tender

Once the purchasing approach and corresponding specification is finalized, the next step is to identify potential suppliers or contractors to invite to tender.

Pre-qualification

Often some form of pre-qualification takes place prior to going to tender. This involves vetting potential suppliers of goods and services to identify those able to meet the required standard. This can be done in a number of ways: questionnaire, supplier site visits, supplier presentations, etc. The most widely used method is a pre-qualification questionnaire, which is particularly useful where a large number of suppliers might potentially be able to fulfil the organization's needs. (See Chapter 8 for examples and more information on the use of questionnaires to qualify suppliers.)

Questionnaires should be tailored to the organization's key requirements. From a sustainability standpoint, what is asked for depends on what the organization has identified as its key issues. However, waste, carbon, raw material/recycled content, water, local labour, labour standards, equality and diversity legislation, employment skills and training schemes are the most common areas examined.

Increasingly, pre-qualification is carried out through shared proprietary industry databases such as SEDEX or Achilles. While these databases may not provide all the answers regarding an organization's specific pre-qualification needs, they can be a useful tool. They typically provide the purchasing organization with a pool of suppliers pre-qualified on specific criteria such as health and safety, environmental performance, and corporate responsibility criteria. They also allow suppliers to respond to questionnaires only once in a standard way agreed by the industry so that this information can then be accessed by multiple customers searching for pre-qualified suppliers, thus reducing the burden on suppliers of questionnaire fatigue.

If suppliers are deselected at the pre-qualification stage, it is good practice to formally notify them and provide some degree of debrief. Suppliers should be made aware if and how their sustainability credentials fell short of the requirement, which in turn should send a clear signal to the market regarding the importance of sustainability.

Issuing the tender

Integrity of the evaluation process is fundamental and all bid evaluation criteria, scoring methodology and benefits assessment should be agreed before any tender is issued. The aim is to ensure an optimum sourcing decision is made balancing social, environmental and economic factors. Criteria can be assessed in a number of ways, including:

- weighting;
- setting minimum requirements or performance standards;
- as part of WLC assumptions;
- monetizing certain impacts such as energy consumption, waste and carbon costs, e.g. the Carbon Reduction Commitment.

Sustainable factors may be given a higher weighting in purchasing arrangements for products and services where the sustainability related risk is greater. This process is led by procurement but it should involve all the key internal stakeholders to ensure continued buy-in and to ensure that a consistent message is given to the market.

The weighting criteria and evaluation methodology should be shared with bidders so the importance of all aspects of the proposal, including the sustainable business requirements, are understood.

Key points

✥ *Suppliers with good energy and waste performance should be in a position to offer lower prices. However, some suppliers with socially and environmentally unsustainable practices might be able to offer prices that are unrealistically low, for example, with poor labour standards. Unless robust pre-qualification, tender processes and evaluation criteria are in place to ensure good minimum standards before the supplier is taken on, the purchasing organization will be constantly undermining its own ethical policies, exposing itself to reputational risk, and giving a signal to the market which undervalues sustainability against other issues.*

4 Evaluate and award

The tender responses should be evaluated in line with pre-agreed scoring methodology. While the specification should always capture sustainable elements in as much detail as possible, there are also other ways to promote sustainable outcomes at the evaluation stage, i.e. after the specification has been finalized.

- Rewarding superior standards and performance. The degree to which suppliers can meet the organization's sustainable requirements might not always be known when writing the tender. In this case, specifications may identify minimum standards and evaluation criteria can then be used to reward performance that exceeds this level. Extra points may be awarded in incremental levels for proposals exceeding the minimum criteria. For example:

  Vehicle carbon emissions:

  o specification: minimum standard <150 g CO_2/km; and
  o evaluation: one point awarded for every 10 g below threshold.

- Qualitative judgements. Suppliers of services may be requested to summarize their experience or provide method statements within their tender response. This allows the evaluation team to assess their approach to sustainability, identify the associated social and environmental risks and develop adequate measures to address them. Other examples include an assessment of the supplier's alignment with the potential customer's organizational objectives, or cultural fit, might be important for some contracts. In this instance, suppliers whose approach is culturally sensitive or most appropriate may be rewarded, e.g. health and social care-related contracts.
- Fit-for-purpose assessments. It is also important to identify and properly evaluate products that might not be sufficiently robust, leading to higher repair and replacement costs. Other proposals might be over-engineered, providing unwanted functionality or service at added expense. Neither extreme provides a sustainable solution and this should be reflected in the evaluation.
- WLC.

Supplier auditing

Buyers may audit their suppliers and prospective suppliers at different points across the purchasing process if there is a significant risk, priority or opportunity. However, as this is typically a costly and resource-intensive activity, this is frequently performed once the supplier or suppliers have been shortlisted at the tender evaluation stage. Assessing supplier operations via tender or pre-qualification questionnaires may not be robust enough for certain categories of spend: those with significant health and safety considerations, environmental impacts, where integrity of sustainable source materials is questionable or where there is potential for worker exploitation. (This subject is examined in more detail in Chapter 9.)

Conducting negotiations and agreeing terms and conditions

Private sector organizations (and public sector organizations under competitive dialogue rules) might have the ability to negotiate following evaluation of tenders. Sustainability considerations should not be traded as part of this negotiation process and care should be taken not to focus only on cost at the expense of other specification needs. However, the supplier can be very responsive at this stage of the process and it might be an opportunity to proactively influence the supplier's future sustainability agenda to improve the extended supply chain performance. It is also an opportunity to secure supplier agreement to take actions to mitigate any supply chain risks and/or reduce those impacts identified in any risk assessment during the earlier pre-qualification or tender evaluation stage.

There might be certain sustainable commitments that could not be delivered through the tender process and these should, where possible, be written into the contract to ensure that the supplier is contractually bound to deliver them. For example, commitments to switch to (or increase the use of) sustainably managed timber, reduce or eliminate the use of a hazardous chemical or ensure improved working conditions further down the supply chain. (In some instances these may be written in a separate supplier improvement plan or a memorandum of understanding, although this would not then be contractually binding.)

Upon conclusion of the negotiation, the supplier is formally awarded the contract, which should be fully approved by the necessary stakeholders and the wider stakeholder community should be informed of the new arrangements. Sustainable benefits should be publicized and both supplier and organizational success recognized; this should be linked back to the procurement and/or organizational sustainable strategy and policy wherever possible.

Example: The Olympic Delivery Authority (ODA) has set high standards for sustainability and all venues are required to achieve a Building Research Establishment Environmental Assessment Method (BREEAM) rating of 'excellent'. The Commission for a Sustainable London (CSL) expressed significant concerns that these requirements were not always being written into contracts. CSL has since recommended that the requirement for an 'excellent' rating be specified in all contracts for permanent venues, even if this means inserting them after deals have been signed.[3]

Another good example from the ODA is the sustainable food and catering initiative which highlights how sustainability can still be included after the contracts have been awarded. Catering for the construction workers is not centrally procured and each tier-one contractor has made its own catering arrangements. The ODA has introduced a Food Safety and Sustainability Scorecard and assesses caterers on an annual basis. This has improved the standard of catering and choice for construction workers.[4] This was not included in any of the contracts but suppliers and their caterers wanted to do it.

Unsuccessful suppliers should be notified and fully debriefed and, at this point, suppliers should be informed if and how their sustainability credentials fell short of the requirement. This in turn reinforces the importance of sustainable business practices within the supply market.

Key points

> ✍ *Further supplier assessment may be needed prior to awarding the contract. This normally happens if there are significant health and safety considerations, environmental impacts, where integrity of sustainable source materials is questionable or where there is potential for worker exploitation. An audit of the supplier facility may be completed by a specialist in-house assessor or by a third party.*

✎ *Sustainability requirements should be captured within the contract as fully as possible.*

✎ *If sustainability aspirations could not be delivered through the tender process, then supplier (or joint) improvement targets should be agreed at this stage (note that if they can't be written in the contract, then the supplier is not contractually bound to deliver them).*

5 Implement

There is a period of transition and bedding in at the start of any new contractual arrangement and frequently the influence and involvement of stakeholders changes as the contract becomes operational. Sustainable requirements and related performance targets need to be understood by relevant internal stakeholders to maintain a consistent message and focus regarding the importance of sustainability.

Finalizing the review process and improvement plans

The supplier review process, key measures and measurement methodology of contract terms should be finalized and agreed. A supplier performance improvement plan which integrates sustainable measures and targets should be finalized and jointly agreed. Note that baseline data gathering might be required before meaningful targets can be defined.

Sustainable targets and other improvement targets need to be linked with the contract management and review process to ensure continuous improvement and sustainability remain firmly on the commercial agenda. Many organizations use performance indicators to measure their own performance and that of their suppliers. Targets and related performance indicators can cover the whole spectrum of sustainable impacts from raw materials sourcing, labour standards across the supply chain, local sourcing and training, through to production, use and end-of-life management. (Measurement is discussed below as an 'Enabler' to sustainable procurement, and in Chapter 10.)

Key points

🖐 *Do not lose sight of sustainability requirements once the contract becomes operational.*

🖐 *Jointly agree how the contract will be managed including the review process, performance targets and measurement methodology, as soon as possible to maximize supplier (and joint) performance. These targets should capture sustainability priorities relevant to this category and your organization.*

6 *Manage performance and relationship*

Ongoing performance monitoring is essential throughout the contract to ensure that the supplier continues to deliver in accordance with the specification, contract terms and/or separate performance improvement plans. A Supply Management poll of 100 buyers in January 2009 indicated that 36 per cent of respondents admitted that they had no formal process for managing contracts. Many indicated this was devolved to individual departments or was handled informally by the purchasing team.[5]

Often organizations adopt a balanced scorecard methodology where sustainability criteria can be monitored alongside service, quality delivery, cost and technical requirements. Should any individual score or combined score show a negative trend or fall below an agreed threshold, the supplier should be required to take corrective actions. Review meetings should be set at agreed intervals and for key suppliers these should be held face to face and should provide an opportunity for both parties to communicate, share concerns, promote understanding and foster a good business relationship. Organizations should consistently attempt to harness suppliers' expertise to maintain competitive advantage and a constructive review process fosters this.

Supplier failure
In extreme cases it might be necessary to exit a relationship with a supplier where the supplier has failed to make the required sustainability improvements.

This should be a last resort and only taken after the purchasing organization has made the effort to support the supplier to meet agreed requirements, but where the supplier has made little or no effort to improve. To continue to source from such a supplier indicates to competitors and other suppliers that the purchasing organization is not serious about its sustainability commitments across its supply chains. Other considerations at this stage might be appropriate, e.g. payments of severance or other steps a buyer can take to ensure that workers get paid before final payments are made.

United Utilities (UU) has a structured supplier relationship process in place which deals with non-compliance. As part of this process, the worst-performing suppliers are identified and an improvement plan is jointly agreed. UU has had some success to date in helping suppliers get better at sustainability. However, if performance does not improve, the supplier could lose UU's business after having its contract terminated. Conversely, UU rewards high-performing suppliers with contract extensions, client references and supports the supplier in new product/service launches and aiming for a closer client–supplier relationship.

Disposal and end-of-life management
Some goods will require disposal strategies to be developed at the end of their useful life which should be in line with any relevant UK and/or local disposal legislation. Disposal options should be reviewed and assessed with the aim of minimizing environmental impacts, maximizing recycling and reuse and determining all opportunities to minimize landfill and pollution.

However, these disposal requirements should not only be considered at the end of the life cycle, but should be factored in throughout the design, procurement process and during operational phases of the product life. This includes ensuring consideration for disassembly and reuse at the design stage, optimum choice of components and materials in the specification to maximize recycling opportunities, and recovery of subsystems and resources while minimizing the use of hazardous materials that could be dangerous and costly to dispose of.

Key points

- ✧ *Managing suppliers appropriately and engaging in supplier or joint improvement opportunities can add significant value to your organization.*
- ✧ *Knowing that major customers continue to treat sustainability as a priority through the life of the contract should also promote confidence and encourage suppliers to invest in process improvements, training, research and development, etc.*
- ✧ *Harness your supplier's expertise for your competitive advantage; use the supplier review process to promote understanding and foster a good business relationship.*
- ✧ *Disposal and end-of-life management should be considered throughout the design, procurement and operational phases of the contract and not only at the end of the life cycle.*

7 Review and learn

Continuous improvement is the cornerstone of good procurement practice. Buyers should ensure that processes are in place to allow review and feedback of key projects and purchases to ensure learning is captured, shared and acted upon. This should be an ongoing process and buyers do not need to wait until the end of the procurement cycle to commence this. The procurement process illustrated in Figure 12 follows the Plan, Do, Check, Act approach (PDCA).

It is also important to understand that reviewing the last project and improving upon it may not be enough. The sustainability agenda is continually evolving and it is important to refresh sustainability knowledge continuously and build this new knowledge into your requirements and practices. For example, in 2008 the EU adopted a new air-quality directive[6] with member states having two years to transpose the new directive. This means in 2010 air quality and its impact on human health became an even bigger issue across urban areas than before.

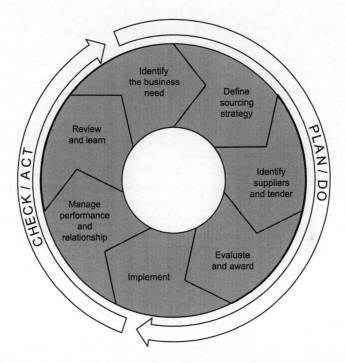

Figure 12 – PDCA approach applied to the procurement process

Enablers

The final theme covered within the 'how to do' sustainable procurement section of the standard is enablers. These are shown as the outer ring of the BS 8903 schematic. Enablers are tools, techniques, skills and ways of working that underpin the procurement process and sustainable procurement activity.

Leadership and governance

This enabler is concerned with whether there is sufficient management support and endorsement for sustainable procurement. Does the right level of support exist across the organization? Leadership can occur at all levels but senior-level endorsement is needed if sustainable procurement is to become embedded in an organization's ethos.

Governance is concerned with whether there are the right systems, structures and controls in place to ensure that sustainability is recognized, considered and resourced throughout purchasing and the wider organization. Accountability is also important: it should also be clear as to who is accountable for ensuring the sustainability for a particular purchase, project or for delivery of key objectives. In summary, good leadership and governance should ensure a consistent and cohesive approach to sustainability which is reflected in an organization's processes and decision making.

> The support of top managers makes a crucial difference as to whether a company can achieve the position of 'best performer' in sustainable procurement – this is even a more powerful driver than legal requirements.
>
> *Green and Sustainable Procurement Today – A Perspective on Leading European Companies.* Supply Chain Management Institute of the European Business School, 2009

People

All staff and stakeholders that have an influence over purchasing decisions need to be sufficiently competent and understand both the reasons for implementing sustainable procurement and their role in making it happen. Competence is a fusion of knowledge, skills and attitude and BS 8903 examines how this competence may be gained through a combination of training, job shadowing, networking (for example, attending conferences), sharing of knowledge and work experience.

Development is not limited to procurement staff and other stakeholder groups must also share a common understanding and alignment of values and sustainable business goals. Training and development may be required which may extend to first-tier suppliers and key suppliers further down the supply chain. Key internal stakeholders may also benefit from further development, for example, training in WLC techniques may help finance and budget holders understand the need to overcome constraints in budget mechanisms where timing of expected benefits may not align with the budget set. Staff need to share a common understanding and alignment of sustainable business goals, so they can work across departments and adopt (and budget for) sustainable solutions that might have longer payback periods over the life of the product, works or service in question.

In short, this enabler is critical as sustainable procurement will not happen if the staff involved in purchasing decision making do not have the necessary skills, know-how and alignment.

Case study

United Utilities (UU) a UK plc based in north-west England, providing water and wastewater services throughout north-west England embarked on a comprehensive development of sustainable procurement in 2008. UU began by providing training to all its supply chain staff in its organizational sustainability goals and how they could make a difference in terms of supply chain management. Staff received a combination of classroom-style teaching, interactive workshops, one-to-one 'surgeries', a 10-strong Knowledge Group and many informal meetings/coaching sessions.

Training of supply chain staff included:

- clarifying the scope and reach of the 12 sustainability themes that UU has identified as important to its operations;
- how to assess the risk and impact of these themes on a category and sub-category basis;
- how to produce six-year category action plans; and
- how to build sustainability into the procurement process, for example, including sustainability questions in the pre-qualification and tender documents, assessing supplier responses and setting supplier improvement targets that align with the overall UU sustainable targets.

Employee opinion surveys across UU over the last three years show a significant improvement in staff perception around sustainability; specifically, UU asks its employees if they know how to take action to make the company more sustainable. In 2008, survey results showed that fewer than 40 per cent scored favourably in the supply chain department; since the introduction of the sustainable supply chain strategy, this percentage has risen to over 90 per cent. This has also contributed to the retention of key talent in the department and sustainability is now a key driver for any new recruitment.

Risk and opportunity

This enabler discusses the need to ensure that procurement staff have the basic skills needed to identify, quantify and then manage potential sustainability risks and opportunities. Buyers need to understand what the sustainable priorities are for their organization and how this translates to a category, sub-category or project level (i.e. what this means for a particular category). There are many techniques that may be used to assess risk and BS 8903 recommends that once risks and opportunities are identified they should be prioritized using a combination of:

- spend;
- scope to make a difference; and
- your influence over the market to affect change.

Note that sustainable risks and opportunities should be managed throughout the life of any contract and form part of supplier management efforts. The business environment is dynamic and, as such, risk should *not* be completed as a 'one-off' exercise. Risk management plans are live documents that should evolve over the life of the contract and in response to changing market and internal requirements. (Risk management will be discussed in more depth in the following chapter.)

Engagement

It seems that the root cause of success or failure of a project to deliver the expected results to the stakeholders often comes down to one item: communication. The ability to build positive relationships with stakeholders, align thinking and communicate in a timely and effective way is crucial.

When considering your sustainable procurement agenda it may be useful to split stakeholders into two major groups: the first group help you to shape the wider sustainability agenda for your organization and include shareholders, political leaders and NGOs. The second group are those stakeholders who will help you to deliver the sustainability objectives that have been set. This second group is primarily staff and suppliers. Buyers must be able to identify and engage with relevant stakeholders at the appropriate time throughout the procurement cycle. All stakeholder groups should be identified at the start of any project and communication/engagement plans should be created and managed throughout. The aim is to promote understanding and enable stakeholders to input into decision making when and if appropriate; this will help to build ownership and commitment to the desired outcomes. There is a broad spectrum of stakeholders in any purchasing decision from internal departments to supply chain partners, through to the communities affected by the resulting purchase or project. Cultivating the right relationships and taking time to build a shared understanding of sustainability goals will pay dividends over the longer term.

Taking a broader perspective, some organizations are taking a leadership role and engaging with suppliers to help them improve their sustainability credentials. Lambeth Council is a good example. Lambeth is the second largest inner London Borough with an official population of 272,000 and approximately 10,000 businesses. The council has taken steps to engage with potential suppliers through Supply Lambeth 2009 – a programme that connects local businesses to council contracts. Through events and workshops the programme assists suppliers in tendering for council contracts. All suppliers that tender must sign up to Lambeth corporate policies, which include an environmental charter, sustainable construction policy and sustainable timber purchasing policy. Lambeth also uses the local government Flexible Framework Assessment to measure supplier sustainability.

In October 2008, Lambeth's Corporate Procurement team established a Key Supplier Network consisting of Lambeth's top 30 suppliers. The aim is to help Lambeth SMEs to become part of these larger suppliers' supply chains. Additionally, Lambeth is participating in 'Supply Cross River'– an initiative involving several boroughs that is designed to open up supply chain opportunities to London SMEs and promote supplier diversity to buyers.[7]

In summary, buyers should collaborate with suppliers and other parts of the business to realize sustainability ambitions.

Measurement

The final enabler is measurement; this is important as you need to know what difference your sustainable purchasing practices are actually making. Measurement is typically applied to purchasing practices and outcomes; these are referred to as practice measures and operational measures.

- *Practice measures*: these are also known as management performance indicators and provide information on the organization's capability and efforts in managing sustainability within its purchasing operations. Examples include the percentage of staff trained in sustainable procurement principles, or number of contracts with sustainability criteria included. The Flexible Framework is a comprehensive tool by which an organization can measure its sustainability practices. As an organization's maturity and competence of sustainable procurement increases, these tend to evolve into more tangible operational-level indicators.

• *Operational indicators*: these tend to be more focused on the actual outcomes of sustainable initiatives, for example, actual reduction in waste sent to landfill, reduction in carbon emissions, water usage, increases in recycled content, number of apprenticeship places offered, etc.

Measurement will be discussed in more depth in Chapter 10.

Summary

This chapter has provided an overview of the main section of BS 8903 'How to do sustainable procurement'. This is represented by the BS 8903 schematic shown in Figure 1 and is further divided into three themes:

1 Fundamentals – these are the higher-level organizational and procurement policies and strategies that should be in place to provide the strategic context and identify the strategic priorities. These should guide decision making and sustainable procurement practice.
2 Procurement process – this is a generic procurement process and BS 8903 identifies the sustainability considerations and activities that should be addressed at various points across this process.
3 Enablers – these include ways of working, competencies, practices and techniques that should be in place and utilized by managers or buyers on an ongoing or periodic basis. These enablers *support* the activities within the procurement process.

The following chapters go on to examine some of the areas that buyers typically want to explore in more depth when managing sustainable procurement.

> ### Useful resources
>
> BS 8903, *Principles and framework for procuring sustainably — Guide*. See: http://shop.bsigroup.com

London 2012 sustainability policy, see: www.london2012.com/documents/locog-publications/london-2012-sustainability-policy.pdf

Sustainable development at Transport for London, see: www.tfl.gov.uk/corporate/about-tfl/8127.aspx

Willmott Dixon sustainable supply chain strategy, see: www.willmottdixongroup.co.uk/careers/our-values-and-culture/corporate-responsibility

BS EN ISO 14001, *Environmental management systems — Requirements with guidance for use*. See: http://shop.bsigroup.com

Government Buying Standards – official sustainable specifications covering a range of products for government buyers; they provide useful information about sustainable procurement and how to apply it when buying, see: www.defra.gov.uk/sustainable/government/index.htm

References

1 'Freezer-free: Owner of Ben & Jerry's launches room-temperature ice cream project', *Scientific American*, 24 August 2009. Retrieved from: www.scientificamerican.com/blog/60-second-science/post.cfm?id=freezer-free-owner-of-ben-and-jerry-2009-08-24

2 'Driverless cars with bug-eyed windows, arriving soon at Heathrow', Timesonline, 12 August 2009. Retrieved from: www.timesonline.co.uk/tol/driving/news/article6792747.ece

3 'Olympic standards met so far', Paul Snell, *Supply Management*, 19 February 2009, p.10.

4 'On your marks, get set, grow'. Commission for a Sustainable London 2012. Thematic review, April 2010. Retrieved from: www.cslondon.org/wp-content/uploads/downloads/2010/07/2010_Food_Review.pdf

5 SM100 Poll, *Supply Management*, 22 January 2009, p.9.

6 Directive 2008/50/EC adopted on 21 May 2008. Retrieved from: http://ec.europa.eu/environment/air/quality/legislation/directive.htm

7 'Mayor of London's green procurement code awards 2009', p.10. Retrieved from: www.greenprocurementcode.co.uk/files/2009%20awards%20brochure.pdf

6. How far down the supply chain should I go?

Introduction

This chapter looks at sustainability risk and opportunity. It discusses how responsible organizations are taking steps to manage risk and assure sustainability across critical supply chains. A user-friendly methodology to help to prioritize risk and opportunity at a category or project level is also provided at the end of the chapter.

Assuring sustainability across the supply chain

Many organizations are recognizing the importance of managing their supply chains in a more responsible way and the main question being asked is how far down the supply chain should an organization go to assure sustainability? There is no single answer here, as this will depend on the size of the potential risks or benefits to your organization.

Most simply risk can be defined as 'the chance of something happening that will have an impact on objectives'. These impacts can be positive or negative, so when completing a sustainability risk assessment positive impacts on objectives should also be considered (i.e. the opportunities).

The first step is identifying any potential sustainability risks or opportunities. This requires a comprehensive understanding of your organization's sustainability objectives and a critical examination of how these may apply to your supply chains. Sustainability objectives usually fall into two broad categories:

1 Positively influencing an impact. These tend to provide 'opportunities' for an organization to make a difference and may be driven by corporate or political targets. For example, reducing carbon emissions, reducing waste to landfill, increasing the number of disabled people employed in the supply chain, etc. They may also be driven by cost related to energy consumption or landfill costs.
2 Mitigating a risk. These tend to be reputation driven. For example, detecting and preventing inappropriate labour standards, pollution incidents or other activities your suppliers may carry out that could damage your reputation.

How far down the supply chain should I go?

To decide how far down the supply chain to investigate it is then necessary to have some idea of the size of the risk or impact (i.e. opportunity) you are dealing with.

For example, a major sportswear manufacturer has recognized that it has a significant risk related to its many garment/fabric supply chains and as such is striving to gain complete understanding, transparency and assurance across those supply chains. The sportswear manufacturer explained:

> 'We know where every garment we sell is manufactured and under what labour conditions, we know where every metre of fabric that goes into every garment is made and under what conditions. We don't yet know where every fibre comes from to make up the material but we are working on it.'[1]

The reason for going to such lengths is the potential for reputational damage should poor labour conditions or excessive profiteering be discovered and exposed. For example, the origins of the cotton fibres used in garments is of interest to the manufacturers because cotton accounts for 25 per cent of the world's pesticides and has a significant impact on ground and air pollution. Additionally, cotton is picked by forced labour in some countries. Man-made fibres have their own problems. Their manufacturing processes can be energy intensive and issues can arise relating to employee safety and the management of waste products. When there are numerous potential risks in the supply chain it becomes obvious why some manufacturers are aiming to trace the origin of every fibre. Organizations that buy clothing, as opposed to manufacturing it, may have less reputational risk at stake (for example, clothing needs are restricted to uniforms or personal protective equipment). These organizations may only choose to trace the chain back to the point of manufacture, others may not address the issue at all. In all cases a robust risk analysis is needed to determine the size of the risk/impact presented by the supply chain and develop the right solution.

The Environment Agency (EA) is another good illustration; it is a major construction client in the UK and must lead by example. As such it must not commission building work with unacceptably high environmental impacts. The EA has hundreds of contracts with small- and medium-sized construction subcontractors and the organization recognizes that it cannot assume that its subcontractors will take a responsible approach to sustainable construction performance. (That is, the EA must own the risk, because if poor practice were uncovered, such as built structures containing unsustainable timber, it would receive adverse publicity and it would be a poor defence to say its subcontractors were responsible.)

Organizations need to understand and map their supply chains in order to identify and develop a deep understanding of the associated risks or impacts and their size. For example, Nokia recognized it needed to gain a better understanding of its metal supply chains and could not ignore concern regarding poor practices at some mine operations around the world. One supply chain of particular concern is coltan; this is an ore that contains the mineral tantalum which is used in many electronic products, including mobile phones. It is mined in relatively few places and has great commercial value. Coltan is mined (legally and illegally) in the Democratic Republic of Congo and has been linked with financing the conflict there. Mining activities that fuel conflict or benefit militant groups are unacceptable to Nokia's high ethical standards and has led the organization to take proactive steps to tackle the issue.

One of the first steps required is understanding the complex supply chains associated with primary metal production, which typically has four to eight supplier layers between Nokia and any mining activity. Figure 13 simplifies this supply chain structure.

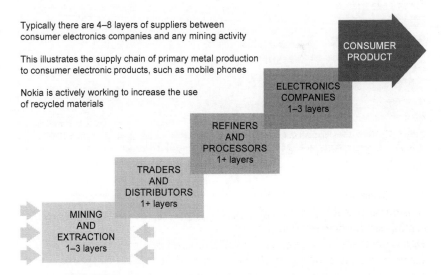

Figure 13 – Nokia corporate responsibility (www.nokia.com/corporate-responsibility/supply-chain)

How far down the supply chain should I go?

At an organizational level Nokia is continuing to improve transparency and support verification of supply chains of metals. Before entering into contracts, it also ensures suppliers meet rigorous health and safety, environmental and labour standards which it requires suppliers to apply to its suppliers. On-site visits to review standards happen on an ongoing basis for a number of contracts and Nokia also works with suppliers on training and support to help them implement and improve standards.[2]

Nokia is also supporting industry-level initiatives such as work with the Global e-Sustainability Initiative (GeSI) and the Electronic Industry Citizenship Coalition (EICC). These groups have conducted extensive research into the key challenges surrounding supply of metals, the ability to trace and track sources of metal used in electronic products and the industry's ability to influence conditions.[3]

Once risks and impacts are identified and the size of the risk/impact is understood, they should then be prioritized to ensure activity is focused across the most critical supply chains. Next, a plan should be developed to address them in a systematic and comprehensive way. Figure 14 provides a summary of the key steps described here and the methodology below provides a user-friendly and straightforward approach to help you prioritize risk and opportunity at a category level or project level.

Organizational objectives
- Clearly understand your organizational sustainability objectives
- What are the key issues and how do they apply to procurement and your supply chains?

Risk/opportunity assessment
- Understand/map key supply chains and identify the main risks and opportunities
- Understand the size of those risks/opportunities and prioritize them to ensure resources and activity are focused where most difference can be made

Risk/opportunity implementation
- Work with stakeholders to identify actions to manage or mitigate priority risks/impacts
- Implement actions and continue to revisit risk assessment to ensure risks are identified as they emerge

Figure 14 – Generic steps to address sustainability risk and opportunity in your supply chain

A suggested methodology

Traditional risk management approaches can be used to think about sustainability and there are many tools and methods for identification, quantification and management of risk already available. Wherever possible sustainability should be incorporated within your organization's existing processes and adding additional or new risk assessment processes should be avoided. This section does not attempt to review various risk management approaches, but aims to provide a user-friendly, simple methodology which, if needed, may help to prioritize and manage sustainability risks and impacts.

Step 1 – Identify risks and impacts/opportunities: think about the sustainability goals and priorities of your organization and/or project in relation to your procurement and identify risks and impacts/opportunities. (Note that it may be necessary to engage with stakeholders and suppliers at this point to ensure understanding of your supply chain and identification of all potential risks and impacts.)

Step 2 – Evaluate risks and impacts: for likelihood of each occurring against the scale of business impact (i.e. would the consequences be significant, moderate or minor?) (see Figure 15). This will help to prioritize the most significant risks requiring action:

- If the likelihood of that sustainability risk/impact occurring is low and the size of the business impact of it happening is minor, you will probably be prepared to *accept* that risk/impact.
- If the likelihood of that sustainability risk/impact occurring is medium and the business impact of it happening is moderate, you will need to take steps to *manage* that risk/impact effectively.
- If the likelihood of that sustainability risk/impact occurring is high and the business impact of it happening is significant, you will need to take steps to *terminate, mitigate or reduce* that risk/impact effectively. (It is possible to terminate the risk by using a different technique or changing the business. A BAA example illustrates this: when an architect for Heathrow Terminal 3 specified a specific type of black granite sourced from Zimbabwe, procurement asked for a different sort of granite to be specified.)

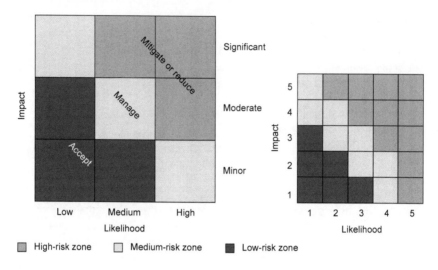

Figure 15 – Risk tolerance model

It's important to define the scales used, i.e. be clear about what constitutes a low, medium or high likelihood and what significant, moderate and minor impacts mean in the context of your business. A major transport sector business does this well; it adopts a similar risk tolerance model that uses a 1–5 scale for likelihood and impact.[4]

Likelihood ratings:
1 = improbable (<10%), 2 = unlikely (10–30%), 3 = possible (30–50%), 4 = likely (50–80%), 5 = probable (>80%)

Impact rating:
This impact (also known as consequence) rating is further divided into categories to reflect the context of company's operation:

1   safety
2   security
3   environment
4   group financial (based on earnings before interest and taxes)
5   business financial (£'s scale can be defined by the business unit)
6   reputation and legal

The safety 1–5 ratings are shown as an illustration:
Safety: 1 = minor injury, 2 = moderate injury, 3 = major injury or chronic health problems, 4 = single fatality, 5 = multiple fatalities[4]

The illustrative example in Figure 16 shows how the results of a risk assessment can be tabulated. This example provides a clear representation of the priority sustainability impacts for each work package of a fictitious construction project. (Note that the sustainability impacts shown here are illustrative; the sustainability risks and impacts considered would differ for each procurement or project depending on the overall sustainability objectives of the organization or project.) The high impacts (as a minimum) should be prioritized requiring further mitigation or management.

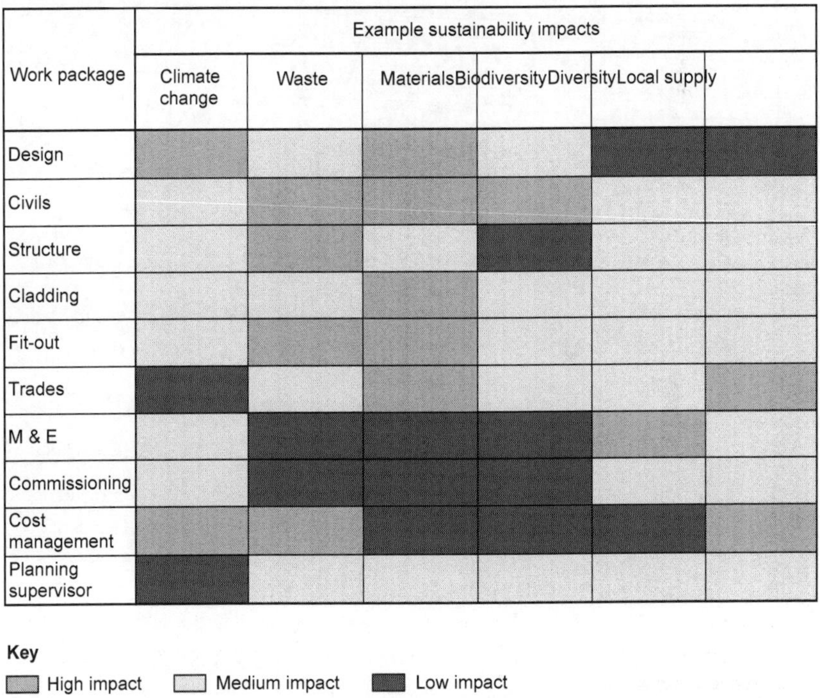

Work package	Example sustainability impacts					
	Climate change	Waste	Materials	Biodiversity	Diversity	Local supply
Design						
Civils						
Structure						
Cladding						
Fit-out						
Trades						
M & E						
Commissioning						
Cost management						
Planning supervisor						

Key

High impact   Medium impact   Low impact

Figure 16 – Illustrative example showing results of sustainability impact assessment against construction work packages

Indirect	Waste (internal)	Carbon	Energy	Water	Community	Air quality		Trade effluent
Travel								
Utilities								
European road freight								
Domestic freight								
Courier service								
Air/sea freight								
Wooden packaging								
Paint shop consumables								
Chemicals								
Construction								
Testing								
Waste removal								

Figure 17 – Second illustrative example showing results of sustainability impact assessment for a high-technology organization supplying energy industry

Step 3 – Further assessment. Typically, the high and possibly some medium risks and impacts will require further action and specific action plans for the risks and impacts could be devised at this point. However, if resources are limited it may be beneficial to complete some further assessment to ensure resources will be focused on the risks and impacts where most difference can be made and hence greater benefits achieved. To do this, risks and impacts may be further assessed against:

• scope to do more in terms of reducing sustainable risks or impacts (i.e. what actions are realistically possible to bring about change and how difficult are they to do?)
• your influence as a buyer to bring about sustainability improvements (i.e. is the power of your spend or project profile sufficient to engage and bring

about changes within the market). This can be a real issue for SMEs which are often unable to exert enough influence over their supply chain.

Step 4 – Develop and implement specific action plans to address prioritized risks and impacts. This action plan should be a live document; it is an integral part of the procurement process and should be updated throughout the life cycle of the procurement. An example action planning template is shown in Table 5.

Summary

Sustainable procurement uses a risk-based approach. To be successful requires a comprehensive understanding of your key sustainability issues and how they affect your supply chains. Note that the size of your risks and opportunities are not necessarily linked to the size of your spend. So, if resources are limited, do not select supply chains for risk assessment on spend alone. Organizations need to deal with sustainability risks at the point in their supply chains where it can make the most difference. The following six tips should help you address sustainability in your supply chain:

1 Be aware of the issues. Sustainability is a constantly evolving agenda and it takes time to address issues in complex supply chains. You need to be up to date with today's issues and have a clear view of things that will impact on your organization in the future.
2 Understand why. If you are not doing this to mitigate a risk or to achieve an organizational objective, you probably should think again. Look for the 'golden thread' back to your organizational goals.
3 Understand your impacts and risks. A robust analysis will lead to a clear understanding of what you are trying to achieve and why.
4 Understand your supply chain. Good purchasers should already know where excessive costs may lie within their supply chain. But what about excessive risk or environmental impact?
5 Make a plan. Plan for the medium/long term and take your suppliers and stakeholders with you. Do not be tempted to find a 'one size fits all' solution.
6 Ensure risk and opportunity assessment is an integral part of the procurement process. Do not treat it as a 'one-off' exercise. Use it as a 'live' tool to identify risks as they emerge and then manage them across every stage of the life cycle of the goods, works or service.

Table 5 – Example risk and impact action plan

Description of risk or impact and consequences for the organization/ project/ procurement	How the risk/impact arises, i.e. root causes	Current risk rating Red/Amber /Green (RAG)	Actions to address risk/impact	Who	When	Residual rating RAG

Useful resources

Sustainable Procurement Task Force, *Procuring the Future*, ch.3, see
www.defra.gov.uk/sustainable/government/documents/full-document.pdf

References

1   'Sustainable procurement – do you go all the way?', Shaun McCarthy,
    Action Sustainability. Retrieved from: www.actionsustainability.com/news/
    80/Sustainable-procurement–do-you-go-all-the-way
2   'Mining of metals from the Democratic Republic of Congo'. Nokia Corporate
    Responsibility. Retrieved from: www.nokia.com/corporate-responsibility/
    supply-chain
3   'Tracing a Path Forward: A Study of the Challenges of the Supply Chain for
    Target Metals Used in Electronics'. April 2010, Resolve Inc. Retrieved from:
    www.eicc.info/documents/RESOLVEReport4.10.10.pdf
4   'HSE Guidance: A Practical Guide to Assessing and Managing Health and
    Safety Risks'. BAA. Retrieved from: www.baa.com/assets/B2CPortal/
    Static%20Files/Assessing&ManagingH&SRisks-May2007.pdf

7. Does sustainable procurement cost more?

Introduction

There is a perception that sustainable procurement costs more and this often prevents buyers from procuring more sustainably. However, buyers need to understand how it is possible to achieve value for money for the customer while also delivering social and environmental benefits for the wider society. This chapter aims to look at some of the issues and show what is achievable. The final part of this chapter provides an overview of whole-life costing (WLC) methodology and uses examples to show how its use can justify more sustainable products that may have a cost premium initially but how cost is recovered through lower-running and disposal costs.

Sustainability and cost management

So, does sustainable procurement cost more? Well the answer is, it depends ... sustainable procurement is not about the cheapest upfront purchase price – it is about delivering value over the life of the goods, works or service. Sustainable business practices (including procurement) are based on the principles of:

✓ consuming fewer resources;
✓ using less energy;
✓ generating less waste;
✓ promoting social benefits; and
✓ reducing harm to the environment and people.

It is about doing business more efficiently and creating true value. This should not cost more and should actually achieve cost saving, and may provide community benefits over the life of the goods, works or service. It's also worth pointing out that the upfront purchase price of sustainable products and services is not always more expensive than traditional alternatives. The typical scenarios a buyer may face are summed up below.

Does sustainable procurement cost more?

a) **Sustainable products with a purchase price that is comparative or cheaper than traditional products; this includes products from recycled sources**

The Olympic Delivery Authority (ODA) recognized that there was an opportunity to improve sustainability by specifying concrete with a lower-carbon footprint. In sourcing concrete for the 2012 Olympic and Paralympic Games, suppliers were given over 12 months' notice that carbon footprint measurement would form a significant part of the tender evaluation, so that they could develop more sustainable alternatives. The market responded and the winning bid was not only the most sustainable but also the most cost-effective. The concrete supplier substituted raw materials in cement with secondary or recycled materials (pulverized fuel ash, blast furnace slag and recycled glass) to develop low-carbon (and low-cost) concrete. Combined with using rail to deliver the raw materials to site, nearly 80,000 tonnes of carbon emissions were avoided, accounting for a 42 per cent reduction against the UK industry average for concrete.[1]

b) **Sustainable products that initially cost a premium**

Using WLC techniques, it is often possible to demonstrate that better value for money will be achieved over the life cycle of the goods, works or service. WLC is not always easy to complete and benchmark cost data may be hard to find, but it is a key economic tool that can help to justify sustainable procurement (this is discussed in more detail later in this chapter).

c) **Sustainable products and services with a price premium attached**

Some suppliers will use the opportunity to treat sustainable products and services as a premium offering to increase their margins. It is the fundamental role of the buyer to challenge this and to use procurement professional skills to drive down cost *and* achieve sustainability. An example from a major building contractor illustrates this point. Its main timber suppliers provide FSC-certified timber at competitive prices compared with non-certified sources. However, the joinery supplier requested a 20 per cent increase for FSC timber. This is not a premium product: it should not cost more, and the buyer was able to negotiate this down. The best way to tackle this issue is to make a policy decision before procurement which does not give suppliers an option – in this situation the seller cannot put a premium on sustainability (this policy-based approach is discussed in more detail below).

d) **Sustainable products and services that do cost more**

In a global, price-sensitive market there is a strong incentive to source commodities from low-labour-cost economies, which may be based on exploitative labour practices. Here the buyer is faced with a moral dilemma: (i) to restrict procurement to developed economies with strict labour and child laws (but ignoring the consequential effects on the economies of developing countries); (ii) to adopt a fair-trade policy which has the potential to drive up prices, but at the same time righting some fundamental wrongs and considerably reducing an organization's exposure to reputational damage; or (iii) just to buy at the lowest price. This is a risk-based and ethical decision, and in these instances it's recommended that the margins made by suppliers should be critically examined. For example, many big-name clothing retailers have been shamed over recent years after uncovering poor labour practices, including use of child labour to provide Western nations with cheap clothing. Despite these organizations' attempts to audit suppliers and insist on commitment to labour standards, this price-sensitive and highly competitive marketplace means that some suppliers continue to exploit their workers. Bhuwan Ribhu, a Delhi lawyer and activist for the Global March Against Child Labour explains:

> Employing cheap labour without proper auditing and investigation of your contractor inevitably means children will be used somewhere along the chain.[2]

e) **There will inevitably be instances where sustainable products and services do cost more, but cannot be justified on the basis of WLC calculations or associated reputational risk**

In these cases there is no mileage in trying to develop a cost- or risk-based justification for buying a more sustainable product. One way to tackle this issue is to make a corporate policy decision, before procurement, that suppliers should not be given an option – pursuing the sustainable option because there is a belief that it is the right thing to do. Elements of Marks & Spencer's 'Plan A' strategy would fall into this group. The return on investment may not be clearly defined but the organization believes it is right, it is what the customers want and that future benefits will be ultimately accrued. An example from the Olympic Delivery Authority also illustrates this. It made a late decision to install ammonia chillers into the air-conditioning system in the Aquatic Centre for the London 2012 Olympic and Paralympic Games. This system replaced the HFC-based system originally planned. HFCs are a potent greenhouse gas with 2,000 times the greenhouse effect of CO_2. The system costs more and it would have cost less for the ODA to pay for carbon offsets. However, the London 2012 bid was predicated on 'the most sustainable Games ever' and on a promise that the London Games will set an example and change behaviour. The Mayor of London and the Olympics Minister made a decision in the interests of contributing to knowledge in the field of HFC-free air-conditioning and using the Olympics as a demonstration project.

Another example relates to Green Works, a social enterprise that recruits and trains the long-term unemployed. This organization channels companies' redundant high-quality furniture to smaller, needier community groups to prevent disposal to landfill. Its customers include a number of banks and well-known corporations, such as Unilever, that are prepared to pay more for this disposal service than they would in landfill costs as this reinforces their environmental and social credentials.[3] A final, everyday, example is toilet paper with a high percentage of recycled material; it is the right thing to buy, as it closes the recycling loop and helps to generate demand for recycled products which is ultimately beneficial to the environment and wider society. In these circumstances an individual or organization has to decide based on stated organizational objectives or personal values whether this represents value for money.

In mitigation, when suppliers have to compete on a like-for-like basis (with absolute clarity on specification), the sustainable option can turn out to be priced less than non-sustainable offerings.

Value for money

Everybody talks about achieving value for money, but do we all know what this means? Money is easily identifiable but value is more complex than many people think. Good procurement, both in the public and private sector, is about seeking best whole-life value for money.

So what does this actually mean? Are we discussing value to an organization or do we take a wider viewpoint such as UK plc or society in general? There is a very fundamental difference between the private sector and the public sector; this must be understood to help understand the concept of value:

- The private sector supplier operates within administrations which set laws determining how suppliers should behave. Different administrations, different laws and different remedies; but the liabilities of the supplier are capped. When the private sector supplier has discharged its legal obligations, then, subject only to its voluntary obligations under a *corporate social responsibility* policy (whether moral, or justified for its long-term economic sustainability) it has no further liabilities to society.
- The public sector cannot ever walk away from its moral and political obligations to society; the social, economic and environmental liabilities are unlimited. The public sector operates under EU law and is always subject to public scrutiny, and officials are accountable to the ministers of the elected government – who can be removed periodically by the electorate.

Therefore, after some analysis of the term 'value' it is probably best to discuss value for money in the context of public and private sector organizations.

Value as a concept captures elements of economics, strategy, finance, management, sociology, philosophy, ethics and, for many people, religion. As individuals we all have different 'values' or priorities and value will always be specific to a person or organization. The following quote sums this up well:

> *There is no such thing as absolute value in this world. You can only estimate what a thing is worth to you.*
>
> Charles Dudley Warner 1829–1900, US writer

This means that each organization and individual will consider 'value' differently; what represents 'value' to one organization may not necessarily represent value to another.

Public procurement

Value for money (VFM) is clearly defined as the primary driver for public procurement. A policy principles document published by the OGC explains that 'VFM usually means buying the product or service with the lowest whole-life cost that is fit for purpose and meets specification. Where an item is chosen that does not have the lowest whole-life costs then the additional "value added" benefit must be clear and justifiable'.[4]

It also indicates that VFM should be assessed over the whole life cycle when considering sustainable procurement options and developing as a business case. This should include disposal (either sale proceeds or decommissioning costs) and take into account all costs and benefits to society as a whole, including the environmental and social benefits and costs, not those simply directly relevant to the purchaser.

The public sector (including some privatized utilities) operates under EU Procurement and Remedies Directives, the broad principles of which are openness, transparency, fairness, competition, and non-discrimination on national and geographic criteria. These principles relate to the treatment of suppliers. So, the basic assumption is that, except in special circumstances the choice of supplier must not be based on the 'characteristics' (policies, behaviours, etc.) of the supplier, but must be based on criteria that relate to the work to be performed or goods required.

Assessment of supplier bids in the public sector should only be conducted in relation to a published set of evaluation criteria, which must be relevant to the subject matter of the contract, and any 'added value' that justifies a higher price must flow from these defined criteria and be assessed from the perspective of the contracting authority. This means that sustainability requirements must be relevant to the subject matter being procured and must be included in the evaluation criteria.[4] The EU directives do allow the inclusion of social and environmental criteria, both in specifications and in the evaluation process, providing they can be linked to the organization's objectives (i.e. making it relevant to the subject matter). For example, if an NHS trust is building or extending a hospital, it is for the benefit of the community and so including economic regeneration criteria (such as requesting building contractors' proposals to train and employ young people or the economically inactive from the community in their bids) would provide added value.

Private sector procurement

The EU Procurement and Remedies Directives are based on fair and equitable competition and most private sector buyers aim to uphold these principles. However, it is not necessary for private sector buyers to adhere to strict bureaucratic procedures around EU procurement law and UK purchasing policy; so buyers need to define what VFM means for their organization or project. Buyers should take their lead from stated organizational (or potentially customer) objectives and goals. Therefore, if climate change mitigation is a stated objective, then any purchasing solution that supports this goal will represent some degree of 'value' to that organization. Where possible, buyers should ensure that the purchasing specification and evaluation criteria are aligned with, and reflect, these organizational aims to ensure that adequate consideration is given to them when making decisions. Therefore, providing an organization has set the right goals and objectives, procurement should be able to determine how 'value' can be achieved from its procurement actions.

As a buyer it is important to understand *why* you are doing something and from a sustainability standpoint if you are not doing it to mitigate a risk or achieve an organizational aim, you should probably think again as it is unlikely to be delivering value to the organization. This does not mean that benefits to the wider society are ignored; it means that it is the organizational objectives and goals that provide this direction. For example, if an organization's business aim is to be a 'fair partner' with a commitment to improving the lives of people within its supply chain and local community, then sourcing activities that provide local employment and training opportunities, such as apprenticeships, should be promoted in the sourcing process to enable the organization to achieve its overall goal.

As in the public sector, when assessing value, the costs over the whole life of the goods, works or service must be considered. While the cheapest whole-life cost (WLC) does not always equate to the most sustainable option, it generally has positive implications for sustainable procurement which often has lower-running and disposal costs.

In summary, to achieve best VFM, whether in the public or private sector, buyers should always try to exploit opportunities for sustainability that bring no additional cost over the life cycle of the goods, works or service.

Whole-life costing – an overview

Life Cycle Costing (LCC) also called Whole Life Costing is a technique to establish the total cost of ownership. It is a structured approach that addresses all the elements of this cost and can be used to produce a spend profile of the product or service over its anticipated life-span.

Office of Government Commerce (OGC)[5]

Does sustainable procurement cost more?

As suggested by the quote above the terms whole-life costing (WLC) and life cycle costing (LCC) are often used interchangeably and this same assumption applies in this chapter. (However, buyers in the construction sector should note that the British standard BS ISO 15686-5, *Standardized Method of Life Cycle Costing for Construction Procurement*, does make a distinction between WLC and LCC. WLC in this standard has a broader scope than LCC.)

WLC analysis is typically used by buyers at either the sourcing-strategy stage to help to decide between competing procurement options and/or at the tender evaluation stage to ensure that contract award decisions are made on cost assumptions over the operational life of the goods, works or service and not just on the upfront capital costs. It is an important tool which helps buyers improve their understanding of the cost structure of any purchases; it also supports cost forecasting and can be used to support scenario modelling, namely performance trade-off against cost.

We need to recognize that WLC is primarily an economic tool, but it often helps to justify sustainable procurement because it takes account of costs associated with 'environmental variables', such as energy, water and consumables. This helps buyers choose between different options on the basis of their environmental impact over their operational lifespan and can demonstrate that sustainable solutions may be more cost-effective over the operational life. We must note that while adopting WLC methodologies is highly recommended, it is not of itself sufficient to guarantee sustainable procurement. It does not take into account the environmental impacts associated with production of the product, only those associated with its use. Taking concrete as an example, WLC assessment of a building that uses a lot of concrete would not take into consideration the embedded carbon associated with its manufacture which has a significant environmental impact. Nor does WLC take into account the type of materials used in production or the social benefits that can be achieved through sustainable procurement.

Figure 18 shows the typical elements that should be considered when completing a WLC assessment.

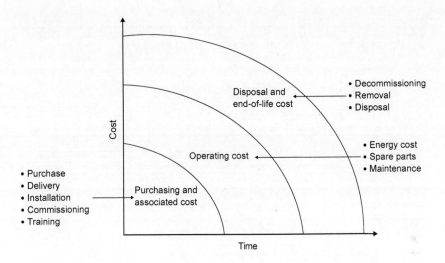

Figure 18 – Illustration of typical WLC elements over time

WLC principles

Three principles are fundamental to complete WLC assessment:

1   An understanding of the cost structure over the life of the goods, works or service (i.e. what costs should be included in the WLC analysis).
2   An accurate method of estimating future costs (such as energy costs, waste disposal costs and costs of carbon).
3   The selection and application of an appropriate discount rate, so that future costs can be adjusted to the present time.

Discounted cash flow

The need to discount future costs is based on the premise that a certain amount of money now is worth more than the same amount of money guaranteed to you in the future. This assumption is based on both the investment opportunities associated with immediately available capital and the interest paid on borrowed money. The public sector employs a discount rate of 3.5 per cent to compensate for the depreciation in future returns on an investment. However, based on a less favourable borrowing position, the private sector must discount at a higher rate, typically around 6 per cent. This is illustrated in Table 6.

Table 6 – Discounting

This table represents the financial savings based on the increased energy efficiency delivered by a sustainability feature in a hypothetical construction. If we assume that the annual associated saving is £10,000 and that the additional capital cost of including the feature was £100,000, it would take 13 years before the energy efficiency savings paid back the investment in the public sector. However, it would take 17 years for the private sector to achieve cost neutrality. Furthermore, we can see that the accumulated saving over a 30-year period in the public sector has a net present value (NPV) of £81,029 as opposed to the private sector saving of £32,186.

Years	Public sector		Private sector	
	Annual discounted saving	Accumulated savings	Annual discounted saving	Accumulated savings
1	9,650	9,650	9,400	9,400
2	9,312	18,962	8,836	18,236
3	8,986	27,948	8,305	26,541
4	8,671	36,620	7,807	34,349
5	8,368	44,988	7,339	41,688
6	8,075	53,064	6,898	48,587
7	7,792	60,856	6,484	55,071
8	7,520	68,376	6,095	61,167
9	7,256	75,633	5,729	66,897
10	7,002	82,636	5,386	72,283
11	6,757	89,394	5,062	77,346
12	6,521	95,915	4,759	82,105
13	6,292	102,208	4,473	86,579
14	6,072	108,281	4,205	90,784
15	5,860	114,141	3,952	94,737
16	5,655	119,796	3,715	98,453
17	5,457	125,253	3,492	101,946

Years	Public sector		Private sector	
	Annual discounted saving	Accumulated savings	Annual discounted saving	Accumulated savings
18	5,266	130,519	3,283	105,229
19	5,081	135,601	3,086	108,315
20	4,903	140,505	2,901	112,216
21	4,732	145,237	2,726	113,943
22	4,566	149,804	2,563	116,507
23	4,406	154,211	2,409	118,916
24	4,252	158,463	2,265	121,181
25	4,103	162,567	2,129	123,310
26	3,960	166,527	2,001	125,312
27	3,821	170,349	1,881	127,193
28	3,687	174,037	1,768	128,961
29	3,558	177,595	1,662	130,624
30	3,434	181,029	1,562	132,186

Source: Appendix 1 *Costing the Future – Securing value for money through sustainable procurement*. June 2008

Key considerations when making WLC calculations should include:

✓ *All costs across the expected usage life and not the physical life of the goods, works or service. (For example, new technology may mean a product becomes obsolete, despite it still being functional.)*
✓ *A careful analysis of what should and should not be included in the cost structure. This is critical, for example, if decommissioning is excluded from some purchases, the results of an analysis could be very different and could result in the wrong decisions being made.*
✓ *Consistency in the application of costs across competing options; if not, this can result in buyers trying to compare 'apples and pears'.*
✓ *Use of sensitivity analysis. It is not possible to predict future costs with certainty, so different scenarios should be created to identify the point at which a different scenario may change a decision.*

Does sustainable procurement cost more?

Table 7 is taken from the 2008 report *Costing the Future*, and it clearly illustrates how different assumptions related to carbon and energy pricing can significantly affect the business case.

Table 7 – Energy and carbon price effects on WLC

This shows how the inclusion of a substantial carbon price and revised assumptions about future energy prices affect the payback period for sustainable construction. The example is based on a case found by the Westminster Sustainable Business Forum's inquiry into sustainability in public procurement of a hospital that had various energy-saving features removed from its design. The environmentally sustainable features were predicted to save £64,930 annually, in addition to reducing carbon emissions by 528 tonnes per year. The reduction in upfront capital costs from removing these features was £944,709.

By revising assumptions about future energy prices, and including a substantial carbon price, WLC shows a payback period of 11 years, after which the features would represent a net saving for the public purse. Without factoring in these considerations a WLC calculation would show a 43-year payback period.

Year	Accumulated energy savings (£)	Accumulated carbon cost savings (NPV)	Total accumulated savings (NPV)
1	£64,930	£32,261	£97,191
2	£129,860	£62,586	£192,446
3	£194,790	£91,092	£285,882
4	£259,720	£117,887	£377,607
5	£324,650	£143,074	£467,724
6	£389,580	£166,751	£556,331
7	£454,510	£189,007	£643,517
8	£519,440	£209,927	£729,367
9	£584,370	£229,592	£813,962
10	£649,300	£248,077	£897,377
11	£714,230	£265,454	£979,684
12	£779,160	£281,787	£1,060,947

Notes:
1 The table assumes rises in energy prices would negate the effect of discounting for the first twelve years of the building's life.
2 The table factors in a saving of £65 for every tonne of carbon emissions saved, applying a 6 per cent discount rate to the accumulated savings.

Issues and barriers associated with WLC

Often there is a lack of benchmark costing data for buyers to use to help inform WLC assessment. This, together with the difficulty of estimating future costs, is a significant problem to the adoption of WLC methodology. For example, buyers need to have access to accurate predictions about future costs of energy as many of the benefits associated with WLC in supporting sustainable procurement alternatives are related to energy efficiency. Energy forecasting is particularly difficult and it is recommended that professional advice be sought to make calculations as accurate as possible. Note also that current and future fiscal instruments will also impact on WLC assessment, such as those associated with the CRC Energy Efficiency Scheme, EU Emissions Trading Scheme (EU ETS), landfill tax escalator and Landfill Allowance Trading Scheme (LATS).

Affordability is another major barrier to adoption of procurement solutions offering best WLC. WLC often advocates a higher-capital expenditure initially to reduce future operational costs; however, buyers often have no responsibility for running costs and the division between capital and revenue budgets prevents transfer of funds to enable more sustainable solutions that provide better VFM over the life of the goods, works or service. Nevertheless, WLC still remains a powerful way of illustrating that the cheapest option rarely equates to the most efficient option, and this tool should be employed to support VFM procurement. The example below is also taken from *Costing the Future* (2008), and it clearly demonstrates how 'affordability' constraints resulted in a 'sub-optimal' purchasing decision.

Case study – Affordability and WLC of biomass boilers in schools

A company was selected to construct eight schools for a local authority. Biomass boilers, expected to deliver annual net savings of £100,000 in energy cost and carbon emissions reductions of 296 tonnes, were initially considered but abandoned due to the short-term affordability constraints posed by the higher installation costs.

Annual energy consumption	10,000,000 Kwh
Plant installation costs	
Natural gas	£507,024
Biomass	£1,312,790
Premium for installation of biomass plants	£805,766
Plant running cost (30 years):	
Natural gas	£20,192,620
Biomass	£12,702,958
Savings on running cost of biomass plants (30 years)	£7,489,661
Total net savings from biomass plants (30 years)	£6,683,895

Notes:
1 Assumes natural gas costs increase by 5 per cent above RPI per annum over a 10-year period.
2 Assumes natural gas costs increase at RPI per annum from years 11 to 30.
3 Assumes annual RPI inflation level to remain at approximately 3 per cent.
4 Biomass boilers are used to cover 95 per cent of the heating load.

Source: *Costing the Future: Securing Value for Money through Sustainable Procurement*. Westminster Sustainable Business Forum, June 2008.

Summary

Sustainable procurement is concerned with doing business more efficiently and creating true value. In many instances over the whole life of the goods, works or service the sustainable solution will be the most cost-effective. Despite this, many organizations still tend to equate the lowest cost with the most efficient outcome and short-term affordability constraints prevent more sustainable alternatives from being procured. Use of WLC methodology should be promoted and buyers should strive to gather the data necessary to inform decision making using WLC techniques; experts should also be used where needed to ensure future cost predictions are as accurate as possible.

In some instances sustainable options may be more expensive even after WLC has been accounted for. In these circumstances buyers need to decide if this additional cost represents VFM by meeting organizational goals and values or enhancing (or protecting) an organization's environmental or social credentials.

Useful resources

Costing the Future: Securing Value for Money through Sustainable Procurement. Westminster Sustainable Business Forum, June 2008.

PD 156865, *Standardized Method of Life Cycle Costing for Construction Procurement. A supplement to BS ISO 15686-5:2008 Buildings and constructed assets – Service Life Planning – Part 5: Life Cycle Costing*. See: http://shop.bsigroup.com

'Measurement of Sustainable Procurement', Adam Wilkinson and Associates, by Adam Wilson and Bill Kirkup, September 2009.

WLC tools

The Chartered Institute of Purchasing and Supply (CIPS) offers guidance on WLC. See: http://www.cips.org/Documents/Resources/Knowledge%20Insight/Whole%20Life%20Costing.pdf

An Excel®-based WLC model can be requested from Forum for the Future in the Sustainable Procurement Toolkit. See: www.forumforthefuture.org/projects/buying-a-better-world

---

References

1 *Towards a One Planet 2012 – London 2012 Sustainability Plan*, 2nd edn, December 2009, p.27. Retrieved from: www.london2012.com/documents/locog-publications/london-2012-sustainability-plan.pdf
2 'Child sweatshop shame threatens GAP's ethical image'. *Observer*, 28 October 2007. Retrieved from: www.guardian.co.uk/business/2007/oct/28/ethicalbusiness.india

3 'Profit with a Purpose'. Jane Simms, *Supply Management*, 31 July 2008.
4 'Procurement – Value for Money Principles', OGC. Retrieved from: www.ogc.gov.uk/documents/20090918_VFM_Policy_Principles.pdf
5 WLC definition. Retrieved from OGC website, see: www.ogc.gov.uk/implementing_plans_introduction_life_cycle_costing_.asp

8. What tools, techniques and skills should I use to promote sustainable outcomes?

Introduction

This chapter looks at how sustainable considerations can be embedded into your procurement process. It will highlight key considerations at each stage and then go on to discuss how sustainability can be incorporated within the specification, pre-qualification, tender and ongoing performance management aspect of the procurement.

It will provide advice and examples to illustrate how organizations are managing to embed sustainability in practice. The EU Procurement and Remedies Directives are referred to. However, this is only in the context of understanding how sustainable considerations may be included in public procurement; a full description of EU procurement directives is not provided. The latter part of the chapter goes on to examine some of the softer skills that good procurers should demonstrate to help promote successful sustainable procurement.

Key considerations at each stage

How and when to consider sustainability throughout the procurement process will require judgement on behalf of the buyer. Each procurement has different sustainability impacts, which means there will be unique opportunities to make a difference. There is no 'one size fits all' approach. Organizations have different sustainable priorities and goals, and these should inform the sustainability objectives and corresponding actions of any procurement.

Once the specification is established, sustainability requirements are usually built through successive stages of procurement. This typically starts with asking for capability in pre-qualification questionnaires, then defining outcomes in the invitation to tender, and finally securing agreement to achieving these outcomes in the contract or order.

Some advice has been covered in earlier chapters (see Chapter 5) and so to avoid repetition Figure 19 sums up the main actions and considerations typically required across the procurement process to promote sustainability.

Identify business need

- Challenge and reduce the demand; is this purchase really needed?
- What are the performance requirements and desired outcomes? Establish business needs, not wants

Define strategy

- Research the market, find out what is available and what is possible. Look for innovative solutions
- Identify sustainability impacts/opportunities. Prioritize these and focus where the most difference can be made
- Use specifications to design in sustainability wherever possible
- Consider use of output-based specifications to promote innovation, letting suppliers meet the need in new ways

Identify suppliers and tender

- Ensure qualification and tender documents capture sustainability requirements
- Keep the process simple and straightforward to encourage SMEs and local enterprises to take part
- Advertise widely and in local media to promote supplier diversity
- Communicate evaluation criteria including sustainability so bidders understand its relative importance

Evaluate and award

- Use WLC techniques where relevant to evaluate bids
- Evaluate and score tenders in line with published criteria which take into account sustainability
- Take time to debrief unsuccessful suppliers, include sustainability performance to reinforce its importance
- Negotiate for sustainability as well as cost; suppliers are receptive at this stage so promote sustainable outcomes
- Finalize contract, agree performance requirements, including sustainability measures/targets, incentives and penalties

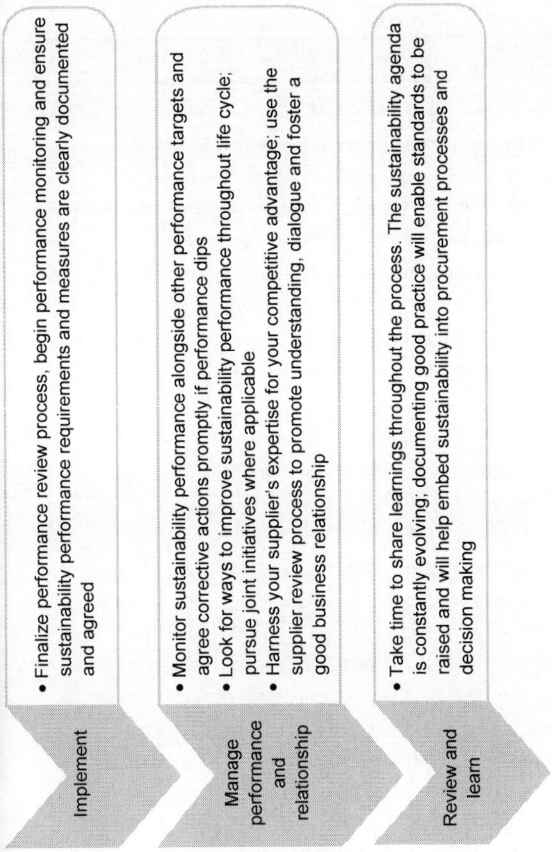

Implement

- Finalize performance review process, begin performance monitoring and ensure sustainability performance requirements and measures are clearly documented and agreed

Manage performance and relationship

- Monitor sustainability performance alongside other performance targets and agree corrective actions promptly if performance dips
- Look for ways to improve sustainability performance throughout life cycle; pursue joint initiatives where applicable
- Harness your supplier's expertise for your competitive advantage; use the supplier review process to promote understanding, dialogue and foster a good business relationship

Review and learn

- Take time to share learnings throughout the process. The sustainability agenda is constantly evolving; documenting good practice will enable standards to be raised and will help embed sustainability into procurement processes and decision making

Figure 19 – Promoting sustainability across the procurement process

What tools, techniques and skills should I use?

This chapter will focus on ways to incorporate sustainability into the specification, pre-qualification/tendering process and supplier management activity. However, often the greatest opportunities to influence sustainability can occur at the start of the process before the specification has been agreed. Therefore, a few key points are worth reiterating:

1   Aim to reduce consumption at the start. As a buyer we must try to ensure that all purchases are really needed and that the demand cannot be met in other more sustainable ways, such as sharing the product or service with others, refurbishing, repairing or upgrading existing assets, switching from disposable to reusable products, or hiring or buying services instead of products.
2   A clear understanding of the business need (and the sustainability impacts related to that need) is fundamental. Pre-qualification (selection), shortlisting and contract award criteria should be drawn from business needs, as, without this clarity, mistakes are likely to be made when establishing the specification and selecting questions to ask at the pre-qualification and tender stage. This could mean that opportunities to reduce sustainability impacts or promote sustainable outcomes will be missed.
3   Challenge the status quo, research the market and know what is potentially available and what is possible. This knowledge should be used to inform the specification. Remember that the sustainable development agenda is continually evolving and new sustainable solutions are becoming available all the time. If possible, tap into a continuous pipeline of supply innovation. If your company does not have a strong R&D resource, it is possible to subscribe to commercially available services.
4   Understand the power of your spend. Be realistic about what is, and is not achievable. Understanding your business risk, sustainability impacts, spend profile and the level of competition in the market will fundamentally influence your procurement approach. If appropriate, use the power of your spend to help to transform markets and create more sustainable solutions. For example, the Swedish government had the courage to consolidate its vehicle procurement requirements to provide a business incentive to encourage auto manufacturers to develop a more sustainable product. The resulting Saab bio-ethanol engines launched in 2005 may not save the planet but it is a great example of using procurement power to create something that did not previously exist.
5   Think about what social and economic benefits could be achieved by your procurement. For example, could this business (or part of this business) help the long-term unemployed, offer employment to disabled people, offer

employment to the local population or help ex-offenders rejoin the working population? Can training or work experience be offered to improve the skills of the labour pool or local businesses? Is this an opportunity to encourage apprenticeships? Can SMEs be engaged? (Research suggests that SMEs in the UK may make a social contribution worth up to £3 billion each year – about 10 times that of large corporations.)[1]

6   Think beyond the ownership of the product and consider all stages of production, transportation, use and disposal when considering sustainable requirements and opportunities. For example, Marks & Spencer has considered the energy consumption of customers when laundering garments and has produced clothing ranges using non-iron and stain-repellent fabrics requiring lower wash temperatures. For the MOD, disposal is a significant consideration: purchasing requirements today must consider long-term future disposal strategies of military equipment, some of which have operational lives of 40 to 50 years.

7   Signal your sustainability requirements to the marketplace early (ideally before commencing any formal pre-qualification or tender activities); this will help prospective bidders to understand what you want and enable them to prepare to meet your needs. The Olympic Delivery Authority concrete tender is a good example. Here, buyers signalled their requirements of low-carbon concrete a year before the tender was issued to allow the industry time to respond. The winning bid was the most cost-effective and had the lowest-carbon footprint.

Developing the specification

The specification translates the agreed business need into a contractual requirement and describes the *specific* needs that are driving the procurement – i.e. the requirements for the services or goods being bought. Capturing sustainability requirements at this point is the *most effective* way of ensuring that sustainability is factored into the purchasing decision. Specifications should be used to establish minimum acceptable performance, actively excluding undesirable features and specifying in positive aspects and preferred higher-sustainability options. Typical sustainability considerations may include:

✓ energy and water efficiency;
✓ use of secondary materials and recycled content;
✓ use of sustainable source materials, e.g. certified timber and timber-based products, construction materials, crops;

✓ avoidance of hazardous chemicals and materials harmful to health in manufacture or use, e.g. PVC;
✓ eco-label equivalent performance standards;
✓ training requirements;
✓ labour requirements (e.g. fair working conditions, health and safety, equal opportunities/workforce diversity); and
✓ reusable packaging/products.

> For environmental considerations, a performance-based definition is often preferable, since in this case the contracting authority does not need to meticulously stipulate all the characteristics that the product/service work should possess, but only the desired effect it should have.
>
> *Buying Green!* Retrieved from http://ec.europa.eu/environment/gpp/pdf/ buying_green_handbook_en.pdf

The specification is the opportunity to define the actual characteristics of a good, works or service, or how it performs. The use of outcome- or output-based specifications are recommended (where appropriate) rather than a detailed technical specification of how the product or service is to be provided. This allows the bidder more scope to innovate, use expertise and find ways to meet the need in more sustainable ways.

Using lighting as an example, the options to promote a sustainable product through the specification include:

• A full technical specification, that specifies exactly what type of high-efficiency lighting is required, i.e. lamp type, dimensions, wattage/energy usage, etc. In this case bidders are told exactly what to provide.
• Output-based specification defining the desired lighting level and energy requirements. This option gives bidders some flexibility to decide how best to meet your needs, but you are likely to get exactly what you ask for and this may result in more sustainable options being excluded.
• Output-based specification that requests the best whole-life value lighting option. This specification indicates only the maximum acceptable energy requirements and minimum acceptable lighting levels. This gives bidders more scope to meet your needs and should harness the supplier's expertise

to provide the best whole-life value solution. (Remember that evidence is important here, as suppliers' salespeople can sometimes make claims that have not been proved.)

- A partnership-based approach can be used. Initial selection may be by one of the methods above but the relationship is longer term (typically more than five years) in which the supplier is encouraged to innovate to meet future 'aspirational' performance requirements. For example, an incentive may be created to share the benefits of improved lighting efficiency over time. Capital investment can be by either party, with a share of the long-term benefits allocated to the party not making the investment.

To improve the diversity of the supply base, further consideration could be given to SMEs when developing the specification. Where SMEs are likely to be competitive or where there is potential to develop SME capability, buyers should consider the scope and scale of the procurement and specify this appropriately. For example, you can encourage SME participation by breaking down work into smaller packages and using brokerage such as meet-the-buyer events and CompeteFor.[2] Alternatively, you can position SMEs lower down the supply chain and encourage tier-one and -two suppliers to engage with them.

Some sustainable purchasing challenges

It is not always easy to determine how to specify goods and services to secure maximum sustainable outcomes from your procurement. For example, there have been cases where favouring local providers is perceived to reduce the carbon footprint of goods and services; however, closer examination of how the supply chain works shows this perception to be invalid. This can be illustrated by one government procurement body that looked at carbon footprint reduction to justify buying local milk. Upon a more detailed look at the supply chain it found that in early 2009 there was no indigenous milk-processing plant, and milk was collected from farms and sent 100 miles to be bottled and then returned!

A similar example comes from IPSERA in Finland. Here a researcher has tried to use carbon reduction to support local food purchase for school dinners in Oulua (inside the Arctic Circle). Schools, however, only buy for 30 weeks per year and so farmers prefer to ship potatoes to wholesalers in Helsinki, whence they are carried back to Oulua!

A final example is that of Scottish-farmed salmon being chilled and air-freighted to China for processing and smoking and flown back to the UK for sale as

Scottish smoked salmon. While this sounds like local produce it has travelled round the world before it reaches your table. The reason, unsurprisingly, is cost: it's cheaper to do it in China!

Other ways to consider sustainability requirements in the procurement process

While the specification is a very important means by which sustainability criteria should be incorporated into the procurement process, it is not the only point in the procurement process where sustainability requirements are considered. There is often some confusion as to how and where in the procurement process it is best to capture sustainability considerations and Table 8 provides some general guidance on appropriate points and methods for including different sustainability criteria.

Pre-qualification

The pre-qualification (selection) stage is used to identify bidders that are acceptable entities to contract with and which have the capability (in principle) to deliver the required good, work or service. At this stage, selection criteria establish the minimum ('must have') levels of capability needed to perform the contract and deliver the business needs. Selection criteria should take account of the particular characteristics of the procurement and associated risks and sustainability impacts. The most common method of pre-qualifying bidders is using a questionnaire (PQQ) and pre-qualification questions should be tailored to the particular procurement. Organizations may help buyers by developing a series of standard PQQ questions for each sustainability impact, enabling buyers to pick a unique mix of questions and criteria to match the mix of sustainability impacts for the product.

Recognized standards such as Forestry Stewardship Council (FSC) certification for timber products or other eco-label performance criteria may be used to define the minimum criteria. (Public sector buyers should use such 'accreditation' brands with caution especially where these are not established across the EU or GATT. Equivalent performance must be allowed for, to ensure that all selection criteria are fair and non-discriminatory and, where possible, it is generally advisable for public sector buyers to outline all performance standards in a full specification.)

Table 8 – Sustainability requirement decision matrix

Requirement	Pre-tender		Pre-award		Post-award	
	Specification	Pre-qualification	WLC	Weighted criteria	KPI[c]	Continuous improvement
Recognized minimum standard (e.g. FSC or ETI base code[a])	✓	✓				
Bespoke minimum standard	✓	✓				
Quantifiable requirement (e.g. recycled content and waste recovery rate)	✓	✓		✓		✓
Requirement can be monetized (e.g. energy, landfill)			✓			
Performance requirement (e.g. reducing energy usage through FM services[b])	✓				✓	
Aspirational requirement (e.g. embedded impacts)						✓

[a] FSC: Forestry Stewardship Council, ETI (Ethical Trading Initiative) base code
[b] FM: facilities management
[c] key performance indicators

What tools, techniques and skills should I use?

Bespoke minimum standards unique to the goods, works or service being procured may also be used as selection criteria (again this should represent the 'must haves' required to perform the contract). Quantifiable sustainability requirements may also be included at pre-qualification stage. However, at this point a buyer should only ask for the minimum requirements needed; this will ensure all suppliers capable of meeting the needs are selected to proceed through to tender stage. An example would be minimum levels of recycled content acceptable in a product.

Qualification can be a time-consuming and costly exercise for both bidders and buyers so it is important that bidders responding to pre-qualification questionnaires have sufficient information about the requirement to rule themselves out early. There is strong evidence that when you describe the requirement clearly at the pre-qualification stage you will reduce the number of bidders that you need to evaluate, saving time and money for both buyers and bidders.

Hints for developing pre-qualification questionnaires

✓ Ensure that information required at the pre-qualification stage is proportionate to the size and complexity of the procurement and the magnitude of the sustainability risks and impacts.

✓ Ensure that every piece of information, document or reference requested is effective in assessing capability and selecting candidates – do not ask for information for 'information's sake'!

✓ Ask questions relevant to the risks, sustainability impacts or opportunities associated with the product or service.

✓ Avoid jargon and paper overload and keep it as simple as possible to avoid putting off SMEs. Provide links or references to more information about specific sustainability requirements. For example, the WRAP website provides comprehensive advice and requirements concerning waste and resource efficiency.

✓ If relevant, ask suppliers to demonstrate their track record in dealing with key sustainability risks and opportunities to achieve VFM.

✓ Don't expect suppliers to do things you are not, but do expect them to share your ambitions to improve.

✓ Try not to inadvertently exclude SMEs. For example, requiring accreditation to ISO 9000 or ISO 14000 as 'must have' pre-qualification criteria may not be appropriate if your likely supplier response will be from SMEs. A lot of SMEs will be diligent in their quality and environmental practices, but they may not have opted for formal accreditation due to the associated cost being disproportionate to the size of their business.

✓ Consider how much you trust the answers – follow-up meetings or supplier site visits may be required.

Example:

At the time of writing Value Wales (the procurement arm of the Welsh Assembly Government) is in the process of developing a Supplier Qualification Information Database (SQuID); the goal is to make the qualification process across Wales more efficient for the public sector and industry. It includes:

- a collection of common, well-thought-out qualification questions;
- a database of answers to these questions supplied by industry; and
- a set of guidance on how buyers should select and use the qualification questions.

It aims to enable:

✓ a more consistent approach which will help industry better understand how buyers will be qualifying them;

✓ industry to be more efficient as the database will store answers to standard questions and allow bidders to reuse any responses they have previously authored for the same question;

✓ public sector buyers to become more efficient at preparing and scoring procurement documentation. This means only asking questions that assess the competence and capability of the supplier that are directly relevant to the contract; (Asking any questions that could be deemed as not relevant runs a significant risk of legal challenge.)

✓ increased competitiveness of the Welsh SME sector by allowing SMEs and local business to compete on a more equal footing as a result of a carefully considered question set that removes some of the barriers for entry for them.

This database will cover all areas of standard pre-qualification questions, including subsections on equal opportunities, sustainability and health and

---

safety. (Note that all questions can be tailored to a particular procurement and additional questions specific to the procurement would also be included in any pre-qualification questionnaire.)

The questions below are a selection of sustainability-related questions from SQuiD to provide you with an idea of basic generic questions that may be asked, along with some critique and guidance for use:

Equal opportunities

Critique	Question	Answer	Guidance
	1. In the last three years, has any finding of unlawful discrimination been made against your organization by an Employment Tribunal, an Employment Appeal Tribunal or any other court (or in comparable proceedings in jurisdiction other than the UK)?	Yes/No	*The buyer may not select a bidder to tender if it has been found to have unlawfully discriminated in the last three years unless it has provided compelling evidence that it has taken robust and appropriate action to prevent similar unlawful discrimination reoccurring.*
	2. If you answered 'yes' to the above question; provide a summary of the finding or judgement and explain what action you have taken to prevent similar unlawful discrimination from reoccurring.	*Text*	
	In the last three years, has your organization been the subject of formal investigation by the Equality and Human Rights Commission or its predecessors (or a comparable body in a jurisdiction other than the UK), on grounds of alleged unlawful discrimination?	Yes/No	*The buyer may not select a bidder to tender if a complaint was upheld following investigation unless robust and appropriate action has been taken to prevent similar unlawful discrimination from reoccurring.*

Critique	Question	Answer	Guidance
	If you answered 'yes' to previous question; provide a summary of the nature of the investigation and an explanation of the outcome (so far) of the investigation. If the investigation upheld the complaint against your organization, provide an explanation of what action (if any) you have taken to prevent unlawful discrimination from reoccurring.	*Text*	
As the bidder may not know at the qualification stage *if* they will use subcontractors and *who* they might be, it is not possible to ask about them directly. In certain circumstances it may be useful to remove this question and address subcontractors at the tender stage when the response to any questions asked can be made contractual.	3. Can you confirm that in the event that you use subcontractor(s) to deliver the required product or service, you will take proactive steps to ensure your subcontractor(s) have taken robust and appropriate action to prevent the reoccurrence of any unlawful discrimination found to have occurred by an Employment Tribunal, an Employment Appeal Tribunal, court, the Equality and Human Rights Commission or its predecessors (or any comparable body in a non-UK jurisdiction) *and* that you understand this may be validated at the tender stage when you are able to identify your subcontractors?	Yes/No	*The buyer may not select a bidder to tender if it does not take proactive steps to ensure subcontractor(s) have taken robust and appropriate action to prevent reoccurrence of unlawful discrimination found to have occurred.*

Critique	Question	Answer	Guidance
This question makes it difficult for SMEs and start-ups to compete effectively; only use it if you are sure it is both necessary and useful. If you intend to score the answer to this question for down-selection purposes, make sure you describe how it will be scored in the bidder's guidance	Do you have procedures in place to protect your employees from unlawful discrimination by other employees or by members of the public?	Yes/No	The buyer may prefer to select bidders to tender that have procedures to protect their workforce from unlawful discrimination.

Sustainability

Critique	Question	Answer	Guidance
	1. Has your organization: (a) been prosecuted in the last three years by any environmental regulator or authority (including local authority) or (b) had any notice served upon it in the last three years by an environmental regulator or authority (including local authority)?	Yes/No	The buyer will not select a bidder to tender if it has been prosecuted or served notice under environmental legislation in the last three years unless there is clear evidence that decisive and comprehensive action to remedy the situation has been taken.
	If your answer to the question above is 'yes' give details of the prosecution or notice and details of any remedial action or changes you have made as a result of prosecution or notices served.	Text	

Critique	Question	Answer	Guidance
	2. Are you in compliance with the Environmental Protection Act 1990, (including relevant Regulations under the Act) relating to licensing and registration requirements concerning hazardous waste?	Yes/No	*The buyer will only select a bidder to tender if they are compliant with the Environmental Protection Act.*
	If your answer to the question above is 'yes' state the licence and/or registration number(s) and date(s) of registration if relevant. If not relevant state 'n/a'.	Text	
As the bidder may not know at the qualification stage *if* they will use subcontractors and *who* they might be, it is not possible to ask about them directly. In certain circumstances it may be useful to remove this question and address subcontractors at the tender stage when the response to any questions asked can be made contractual.	3. Can you confirm that in the event that you use subcontractor(s) to deliver the required product or service, you will take proactive steps to ensure your subcontractor(s) have not been prosecuted or served notice under environmental legislation *and* that you understand this may be validated at the tender stage when you are able to identify your subcontractors?	Yes/No	*The buyer may only select a bidder to tender if it takes proactive steps to ensure subcontractor(s) have not been prosecuted under environmental legislation.*
Only include this question if social benefits are a core part of the requirement and the buyer has the relevant powers to include social clauses.	4. Do you undertake that if you are successful you will: • Advertise appropriate subcontract opportunities on Sell2Wales. • Work with the WAG's Supplier Development Service to open up subcontract opportunities for Wales-based suppliers, especially SMEs, third-sector organizations and supported businesses. • Apply payment conditions to subcontractors that reflect the prime contract from the Buyer.	Yes/No	*The buyer may prefer to select bidders to tender if they are proactive in providing opportunities to local organizations.*

Critique	Question	Answer	Guidance
Only include this question if social benefits are a core part of the requirement and the buyer has the relevant powers to include social clauses.	5. Do you undertake that if you are successful you will: • Consider opportunities for community benefits such as the recruitment and training of economically inactive and disadvantaged people.	Yes/No	*The buyer may prefer to select bidders to tender if they are proactive in providing opportunities to economically inactive and disadvantaged people.*
This question in some ways achieves very little at the selection stage as it is not enforceable and is not readily auditable. However it may be useful in that it shows the buyer's commitment to supporting SMEs through the procurement process.	6. The buyer may include as a contract term a clause requiring you to pay all suppliers and subcontractors within agreed timescales. Would you be happy to comply with such a term?	Yes/No	*The buyer may prefer to avoid awarding contracts to bidders that fail to pay suppliers on time.*

Private sector organizations are also recognizing the need to standardize and simplify qualification procedures to make it easier for small businesses to compete for contracts to supply large global companies. IBM, Pfizer, Citigroup, Bank of America, UPS and AT&T are among major US organizations that have formed a consortium, which has created a website designed to standardize and simplify the application process required for small- and mid-sized US suppliers.

The 'Supplier Connection' website is expected to launch in the first quarter of 2011. It will help suppliers to compete for nearly $150 billion in contracts collectively awarded by those companies annually. This online service aims to reduce time, money and expertise requirements that can deter smaller suppliers pursuing business with a single large company by providing potential vendors with a single, streamlined electronic application form, which they need only complete once. Suppliers will not only have the opportunity to reach US markets, but could also sell to nearly 200 countries – the number of places worldwide where the participating companies operate.[3]

Tender

The specification should always capture sustainable elements in as much detail as possible. However, sustainability impacts can form part of the evaluation criteria providing that the impact can be quantified. For example, the ODA had carbon as 25 per cent of the evaluation criteria within the tender for concrete. It is possible to do the same with other measureable impacts such as waste, particulates, NOx emissions and employment issues such as apprenticeships. Risk can also be used; tenders can be risk evaluated (including sustainability risks/impacts) and points awarded to those bids with lower-risk supply.

Other ways to promote sustainable outcomes at the tender evaluation (award) stage:

- rewarding superior standards and performance. The degree to which suppliers can meet the organization's sustainable requirements might not always be known when writing the tender. In this case, specifications may identify minimum standards and evaluation criteria can then be used to reward performance that exceeds this level. Extra points may be awarded in incremental levels for proposals exceeding the minimum criteria;
- qualitative judgements;
- fit-for-purpose assessments;
- WLC (see previous chapter).

These have been discussed in Chapter 5 and WLC in Chapter 7 and will not be repeated here.

Note that public sector buyers must abide by the public procurement directive of 2004 (Directive 2004/18/EC and Directive 2004/17/EC) and the Regulations that implement them in the UK (the Public Contracts Regulations) which draw distinctions between selection, shortlisting and contract award criteria and govern their use in the procurement process. Contracts may be awarded on the basis of lowest price or the most economically advantageous tender (MEAT), a combination of price and other factors which are relevant to the goods, services or works being procured. Using MEAT (best VFM approach) provides scope to consider relevant sustainability issues. Sustainability award criteria can be used, provided that they:

- relate only to the subject matter of the contract; (This constrains the procurer's ability to take account of an issue at award stage which has not been addressed in the specification. Once again this demonstrates the importance of ensuring that the business need, specification, selection,

shortlisting and contract award criteria are aligned to ensure that all elements are related to the subject matter of the contract.)
- comply with EU law, in particular the fundamental principles of transparency, equal treatment and non-discrimination;
- help identify the bid that represents the best VFM for the contracting authority.

Suppliers may be excluded on the basis of a previous conviction associated with grave professional misconduct or a breach of environmental law.

Contract award criteria must be weighted according to their relative importance. Contracting authorities are free to choose both their award criteria and the weighting attached to them, provided that the weightings enable an evaluation of the MEAT. While these are rules for public sector procurement they also represent good procurement practice for the private sector.

Contract

During this phase the sustainability criteria outlined in the specification need to be translated into contract conditions. Sustainability requirements/clauses must be unambiguous and non-discriminatory. Performance incentives and penalties (which include sustainability performance) should also be agreed. Buyers must be mindful of operating within existing terms and conditions. If an organization has standard conditions relating to sustainability in its contract template, buyers should make sure that these are the ones used when entering into a contract with a supplier. (Or as a minimum, legal advice should be sought if a decision is taken to deviate from standard terms.) Some examples of category-specific clauses which relate to sustainability are shown below.

Construction and facilities management:

- operations shall be conducted between the hours of 9 a.m. to 5 p.m., so as to avoid noise and disruption to the community;
- at least 75 per cent of construction material to be used on site should be recycled and recyclable if and when the building is demolished;
- at least 20 per cent of the employees conducting work must be apprentices;
- construction shall be conducted in accordance with the Considerate Construction Scheme; and
- construction shall be conducted according to the BREEAM Excellent Standard.

Paper and printing:

- all printing shall use 100 per cent recycled paper;
- all printing shall be double-sided; and
- all paper used in printing should at least conform to the standard stipulated under the FSC mixed-source standard or similar. If paper is not certified under the FSC scheme or equivalent, other evidence of chain of custody must be provided.

Transport:

- goods shall be transported in bulk;
- goods shall be delivered outside peak traffic times to minimize the contribution of deliveries to traffic congestion; and
- all packaging used in the transportation of goods shall be returned to the supplier and recycled or reused.

Private sector organizations might be able to negotiate with bidders following evaluation of tenders and before awarding the contract (note that public sector organizations have limited powers to negotiate under competitive dialogue rules only). This is often a good opportunity to influence the supplier's future sustainability agenda to improve the extended supply chain performance. It is also an opportunity to gain supplier agreement to take action to mitigate any risks or impacts that may have been identified during the pre-qualification and tender evaluation stages. Try to ensure that any sustainability commitments or goals that were not delivered through the tender are written into the resulting contract. If suppliers are reluctant to do this, try to capture these agreements in a supplier improvement plan or memorandum of understanding (although these are not contractually enforceable).

Managing supplier performance

Sustainability measures and performance targets should form an integral part of the overall supplier performance management process. Specific performance requirements are typically measured using key performance indicators (KPIs); these measure ongoing performance and are reviewed/reported on at regular intervals. KPIs help an organization/project define and evaluate how successful it is in terms of making progress towards its long-term goals.

Sustainability may also be promoted through continuous improvement initiatives. Here, ongoing performance targets may not be set but both the supplier and customer have jointly agreed to take actions to improve performance above current levels. Any improvements should be quantifiable; examples could include waste recovery rates, recycled content and use of sustainably sourced raw materials. Longer-term or aspirational sustainability goals may also be promoted through continuous improvement initiatives. These goals may not be included in the tender requirements for a number of reasons, such as: the issue may not be well understood (e.g. embodied water), there is inadequate current capability or capacity in the supply market or the customer has been unable to clearly define its long-term requirements at the pre-qualification and tender stage, e.g. carbon measurement across its supply chain. (Note: Measurement is covered in more detail in the following chapter.)

Use of soft skills to promote sustainable outcomes

The soft skills used by a buyer to enable more sustainable procurement outcomes are often undervalued. They are, however, as important (if not more important) than understanding the procurement tools and techniques which support sustainable procurement.

Communication – these skills are essential to ensure that suppliers understand your requirements and goals. However, successful communication must be a two-way process; active listening skills enable a buyer to understand, interpret and evaluate information from suppliers, the wider supply market and customers and translate these into potential sustainable opportunities.

Collaboration – buyers should not act in isolation; stakeholders should be engaged and buy into any proposed procurement strategies, the procurement process and resulting sourcing decisions. This is essential to ensure ongoing support and an aligned approach. Good buyers will collaborate, use team-building skills and influencing skills to help to ensure talent and expertise is harnessed early in the procurement process where the most difference can be made. It is human nature to feel more comfortable with tried-and-tested solutions and suppliers, yet moving towards a more sustainable business model will require everyone to be open minded, receptive to new ideas, and good buyers will be able to overcome barriers to progress, influence key stakeholders and bring everyone on board with sound sustainable procurement proposals.

Judgement – sustainable procurement uses a risk-based approach which requires a systematic evaluation of the impacts and opportunities. However, in the absence of 'perfect knowledge', sound judgement, a degree of intuition and an understanding of the issues can help ensure that all sustainability priorities are identified and prioritized effectively. This should ensure efforts are focused on the areas where there is most scope to make a difference.

Negotiation – is a skill typically associated with general procurement. Buyers should use negotiation skills to secure all procurement requirements identified by the business; this will include sustainable business goals which should not be traded in favour of short-term price reductions. A good buyer should procure sustainable solutions that offer equal or better value over their life than traditional alternatives.

Cultural fit – is also important; this is relevant at both individual and organizational levels. Staff will feel more motivated (and ultimately perform better over the long term), if the organizational values match their personal values. This match should also help reduce staff turnover and retain talented staff.

Gaining a compatible cultural match between organizations is also relevant; this should enable the relationship to be managed in a positive, forward-looking way. Organizations with different values and ethics are unlikely to work productively and in a way that maximizes all opportunities to promote more sustainable business solutions. Such organizations have different priorities and business drivers which will typically mean a lack of alignment, resulting in opportunities potentially being missed. As such, forward-thinking purchasing organizations will struggle to make sustainability goals a reality if their first-tier suppliers are not supportive or do not understand the overriding sustainability ambitions of their customers. A good example is health and social care contracts: the supplier needs to be culturally sensitive to the customer base that it serves. In such cases an aligned understanding and tailored approach can drastically improve the effectiveness of care.

Summary

This chapter shows that opportunities to incorporate sustainability exist throughout the procurement process. Early in the process is a *major point* to influence the sustainability of the procurement and the resulting specification is an essential way of ensuring sustainability considerations are delivered in the final contract. However, once the specification is agreed, sustainability requirements are usually built through successive stages of procurement. Starting with asking for capability in pre-qualification questionnaires, then defining outcomes in the invitation to tender, and finally securing agreement to achieve these outcomes in the contract or order.

The qualification and tender process must be managed to ensure that sustainability requirements are properly captured and evaluated alongside the other considerations of cost, quality, technology and service, etc. Jointly identifying relevant sustainability measures and ongoing performance targets as part of your supplier management process will help to ensure that sustainability performance is maintained, opportunities to improve performance are not missed and that the supplier's expertise is harnessed.

Buyers also need to understand that soft skills play an important role in securing sustainable outcomes from procurement. Good communication, collaborative and influencing skills are valuable. Sound judgement and the ability to negotiate to secure all organizational needs from your procurement are also fundamental skills that a competent buyer should be capable of demonstrating.

Useful resources

Government Buying Standards (formerly known as Buy Sustainable Quick Wins) provide advice to government buyers to buy sustainably. They include:

- 'official specifications that all government buyers must follow when procuring a range of products;
- information about sustainable procurement and how to apply it when buying; and
- direct links to websites with lists of products that meet the standards.'

See: www.defra.gov.uk/sustainable/government/advice/public/buying/index.htm

Green Public Procurement (GPP) provides advice to public purchasers to help them take account of environmental factors when buying products, services or works. See: http://ec.europa.eu/environment/gpp/index_en.htm

Advice on EU procurement

EU Treaty principles – see: http://ec.europa.eu

'EU Procurement Guidance: Introduction to the EU Procurement Rules'. OGC. See www.ogc.gov.uk/documents/Introduction_to_the_EU_rules.pdf

Advice on engaging SMEs

Business in the Community – 'Engaging SMEs in community and social issues'. See: www.bitc.org.uk/resources/publications/engaging_smes.html

OGC – 'Small Supplier Big Opportunity. Flagging your contracts to SMEs'. See: www.ogc.gov.uk/documents/Contract_Flagging.pdf

'Accelerating the SME economic engine: through transparent, simple and strategic procurement'. See: www.ogc.gov.uk/documents/Accelerating_the_SME_Economic_Engine.pdf

OGC – 'Smaller supplier… better value?' Retrieved from: www.ogc.gov.uk

Value Wales – A New Supplier Qualification Information Database (SQuID), to be hosted on the relaunched Sell2Wales website in 2011. The aim is that all of the *common core* questions sought at the early stages (selection stage) of procurement processes will be stored on the system. This should help to save time and cost and reduce the barriers that limit access to public sector procurement opportunities, especially for SMEs.

References

1   'Engaging SMEs in community and social issues'. Business in the Community, July 2003. Retrieved from:
    www.bitc.org.uk/resources/publications/engaging_smes.html
2   CompeteFor is a free service that enables businesses to compete for contract opportunities linked to the London 2012 Games and other major public and private sector buying organizations, such as Transport for London (TfL), Crossrail and the Metropolitan Police. See: www.competefor.com
3   'Small Business Gets a Boost with Supplier Website'. *Supply Management*, 16 September 2010, Helen Gilbert. Retrieved from: www.supplymanagement.com/news/2010/small-business-gets-a-boost-with-supplier-website

9. Standards, codes of practice and auditing – are these enough to assure sustainability within your supply chain?

Introduction

Organizations are coming under ever greater scrutiny by various stakeholder groups (including NGOs, investment analysts, consumers, employees and competitors) who are increasingly evaluating their commitment to ensuring a fair and equitable working environment, environmental responsibility and transparent business practices.

This climate means that your organization will be called upon more and more to demonstrate its social and environmental responsibility. Assurance is likely to become more important. For example, London 2012 aims to be the most sustainable Olympic and Paralympic Games ever staged. To live up to this promise, the Commission for a Sustainable London 2012 has been established to provide independent assurance to the Olympic Board and the public on how the bodies delivering the Games and its legacy are meeting their sustainable commitments. This is the first time such an assurance body has been set up. (See www.cslondon.org for more information.)

This chapter examines how useful and effective standards, codes of practice and inspection regimes (i.e. audits) are, and whether they can provide assurance that business practices within your supply chains are in line with your organization's stated corporate social responsibility (CSR) intentions. It also provides some basic advice which may help you to identify which suppliers or supply chains to examine. The latter part of the chapter discusses other ways purchasers can help to promote responsible practices and assurance within the most vulnerable supply chains.

Public and private sector buyers are able to use standards and codes of practice as a means of assurance; however, public sector buyers need to be aware that there are pitfalls around accreditation, use of codes or standards and inspection regimes where there is not a universal (or at least EU) acceptance of the particular code or standard. Buyers in the public sector also need to be clear that any accreditation or inspection regime should sit alongside an acceptable standard or criteria. Labour standards are discussed in some detail later in the chapter. Again, buyers need to be aware that not all procurements have labour practice issues, and there isn't a universal view on what you should do about it within the public sector.

Codes of conduct and industry standards

Codes of conduct refer to an expected way of behaving. Standards refer to a particular level that a supplier has achieved. Typically, there are social standards relating to labour practices and working conditions. There are also environmental standards relating to environmental performance and environmental management.[1] Codes of conduct and standards in the context of supply chains are similar, and so these terms are often used interchangeably. Codes and standards can be subdivided in several ways:

➤ those which are based on minimum international standards (e.g. UK Competition Commission's Grocery Supply Code of Conduct) and those which go beyond (e.g. SA8000).[2] In some areas this is increasingly blurred;
➤ those which are independently verified (e.g. Fairtrade and EMAS);
➤ Those which apply to an organization (e.g. ISO 14001) and those which apply to a product (e.g. EU Flower);
➤ those which involve supplier representatives and worker representatives in the setting of and governance of the standard (where appropriate to the objectives of the standard), which enables the standard to be improved.

In the context of this chapter an audit can be described as a process to assess a supplier's systems, processes and business practices to establish the validity and reliability of information provided to the customer organization. From a sustainable procurement perspective supply chain audits are used to verify if the supplier organizations are consistently meeting (or are capable of meeting) stated environmental, social and economic requirements which would normally be set out in the tender process and incorporated in the contract conditions.

Why are standards, codes and audits needed?

The scale and breadth of international sourcing is continuing to increase and as a result many supply chains are becoming long and complex. This means it can often be difficult for buyers to gain visibility and a comprehensive understanding of the business practices and the environmental performance of organizations further down the supply chain. Social concerns over health and safety, pay and working conditions, use of child labour, discriminatory/unfair treatment and lack of worker rights, together with unsustainable environmental practices, are the most common causes for concern. Sourcing from developing countries is widespread, and cheap labour and poor working conditions/practices are commonplace; and, while most governments in those countries have ratified the relevant ILO conventions for labour standards, they are often not enforced effectively and sanctions for non-compliance are weak. For example, drinks giant Diageo indicated in its 2010 Corporate Citizen Report that its highest-profile supply chain risks are those surrounding non-compliance with social and ethical standards.[3] Poor labour conditions exist in the UK and EU, too, for example, building projects and retail suppliers have been exposed for very poor labour standards in the past two years.

Many organizations deal with this by requiring suppliers to commit to codes of business conduct and environmental management systems which reflect their stated organizational CSR commitments. These commitments would normally form part of the pre-qualification or tender evaluation criteria and be written into the conditions of any subsequent contract.

However, gaining such assurances from immediate suppliers may not always be enough to prevent socially and environmentally unacceptable practices from happening either at tier-one level or further down the supply chain. Such practices, if exposed, could cause serious reputational (and ultimately financial) damage to your organization or its brands, irrespective of any contractual commitments that may have been made. In short, this is a problem that is refusing to go away, and which must be dealt with proactively. Purchasing organizations need to consider the wider perspectives of their businesses and should manage these risks and opportunities in an appropriate way. For some supply chains reliance on supplier questionnaires may not be enough. Auditing is the most common means of gaining such assurance and should involve *in situ* checking of the supplier's conditions and practices. (Ideally, off site checking or interviews with workers and ex-workers in places where they are free to speak honestly should also be completed for social auditing).

The International Labour Organization (ILO) estimates that there are more than 200 million children working throughout the world, many full-time. They are deprived of adequate education, good health and basic freedoms. Of these, 126 million – or one in every 12 children worldwide – are exposed to hazardous forms of child labour, work that endangers their physical, mental or moral well-being.

The following sections look at the use of codes of conduct and at the role of auditing and discusses if these are really enough to bring about progress within more vulnerable supply chains.

> It takes much more than an annual supplier questionnaire to make progress.
>
> Fiona Dawson, Sustainability Adviser, Forum for the Future[4]

When should auditing take place and how do I determine which suppliers to audit?

Auditing may take place at various points within the procurement process. However, audits are often performed once prospective suppliers are shortlisted at the tender evaluation/award stage. For less critical categories of spend, a supplier self-assessment may be sufficient, but for purchases with significant social or environmental concerns it is usual practice to complete a more detailed audit. Periodic audits may also form part of the post-contract relationship management.

To assess which supply chains to audit and how far down a supply chain it is necessary to evaluate will depend on:

- your organization's sustainability ambitions;
- its perception of risk; and
- gaining an understanding of the size of the potential risk you may be dealing with (this was covered in more detail in Chapter 6).

Building up a supply chain map can help you to assess risk, as it will help to improve understanding of production processes and their associated labour intensity and environmental impacts. This will help to identify what the potential risks are and locate where in the supply chain they lie. To understand more complex supply chains, buyers may need to work with internal colleagues, suppliers, trade associations and other experts to build up a comprehensive supply chain map. Not only does this mapping exercise help to establish the extent of risk and identify points in the supply chain where auditing or further assurance may be required, it may also identify potential opportunities to improve environmental/social performance of the supply chain and identify areas where further support may be required. For example, Cadbury commissioned the Institute of Development Studies and the University of Ghana to map the supply chain of cocoa farming in Ghana, the world's second largest source of cocoa. The study examined the current state of farming and identified the potential social and economic obstacles that may face the country's 720,000 cocoa farmers. The study also suggests solutions to address the issues facing production of Ghanaian cocoa which requires ongoing investment and support to secure its long-term sustainability and to improve the livelihoods of its cocoa farmers.[5]

Industry initiatives, standards and codes of practice

Many codes of conduct and standards exist, covering labour standards, environmental standards (e.g. ISO 14001 and EMAS management) and industry practice (e.g. GlobalGAP which is based on good agricultural practice). Many large purchasing organizations have also developed their own codes of conduct and monitoring systems. However, this has resulted in some suppliers being audited time and again by different customers with similar requirements which can be both time-consuming and expensive for both the buyer and supplier. To reduce supplier confusion and audit fatigue, and improve practice efficiency, there have been a number of initiatives to promote collaboration and sharing of audit data. The *Supplier Data Exchange* (SEDEX) is a good example. It is a membership, not-for-profit organization that enables suppliers to share ethical information and audit data about their sites with customers.

Another initiative is the *Global Social Compliance Programme* (GSCP) which has been set up to allow building of consensus on best practice in labour standards and environmental practices in the supply chain to develop a single, clear and consistent message for suppliers. This harmonization should free up purchasing organizations and their suppliers to concentrate on the identification of root causes of non-compliance and implement actions to address these issues. The GSCP provides an overarching reference framework, and is not another monitoring initiative or a substitute for existing systems; this means it does not undertake accreditation or certification activities. Figure 20 outlines the programme's benefits.

Achilles Global is a commercial organization which collates, validates and updates information given by suppliers on behalf of major organizations worldwide. Achilles offers a range of identification, qualification, evaluation and monitoring services covering economic, environmental, social and ethical

---

For suppliers • Clarity and consistency in labour and environmental requirements • Fewer audits with a focus on building capacity • Time and resources to reinvest in production quality	**For purchasing companies** • Simpler buying • Lower complexity and cost • More resources for remediation • More leverage through critical mass • More effective risk management • Exchange of best practices

For workers	
• Clear understanding of their rights • Effective communication channels • Ability to address grievances	• Improvement of working conditions • Ability to raise issues directly with purchasing companies

For existing initiatives • Exchange and integration of best practices across all sectors and at a global level • Increase reach and value for members • Transparency and comparability	**For civil society stakeholders** • Guide corporations on critical issues • Provide advice and constructive support on the strategic direction of the GSCP • Monitor and evaluate progress • Provide guidance on remediation

Figure 20 – Shared benefits of the Global Social Compliance Programme (www.gscpnet.com)

requirements. Its supplier management services require suppliers to complete a pre-qualification questionnaire which, after verification, means the supplier's details can be shared with buyers in that same sector. For buyers, Achilles provides a means to identify, qualify, evaluate and monitor supplier information; this includes physical audits of high-risk and/or critical suppliers.

In conjunction with key buyers, Achilles has developed the Achilles Carbon Reduction Programme *CEMARS* (Certified Emissions Management and Reduction Scheme) for suppliers to measure, manage and report on their organizational carbon footprint. CEMARS includes an audit to validate supplier information and enables suppliers to justify claims about emissions and reduction plans with verified information. Buyers can use CEMARS information to gain visibility of carbon-related supply chain risk, make informed purchasing decisions and meet sustainable procurement goals.

E–TASC (Electronics – Tool for Accountable Supply Chains) is an example of a sector-specific scheme. This is a web-based system for information and communications technology (ICT) companies to manage corporate responsibility throughout their supply chains in an efficient way. E–TASC contains a tool to

---

help members conduct an initial risk assessment of suppliers before proceeding to the more in-depth self-assessment. It is based on high-level information about the type of supplier, activity and country of operation. For the more in-depth assessment suppliers fill in a single questionnaire on E–TASC, addressing ethics, labour rights, health and safety, and environmental aspects. Suppliers can also share their responses with multiple participating customers, rather than completing separate assessments from different companies.

When using standards, the most important issue for buyers is to ensure that you know what the standard requires, that this is communicated properly to your suppliers and that they clearly understand the requirements.

Purchasing organizations are also requiring their suppliers to implement an environmental management system (EMS). This is a structured and documented system which manages a business's environmental performance and responsibilities. EMS is a risk management tool and all EMS standards have a similar framework, which can be applied to any private or public sector organization.

There are five main recognized standards in relation to environmental management:

1 ISO 14001:2004 international standard for environmental management;
2 Eco-Management and Audit Scheme (EMAS);
3 IEMA Acorn Scheme;
4 BS 8555:2003, *Environmental management systems — Guide to the phased implementation of an environmental system including the use of environmental performance evaluation;*
5 Green Dragon (Arena Network).

> The main rationale for the creation of ISO 14001 was that its worldwide acceptance should facilitate international trade by harmonizing otherwise diffuse environmental management standards and by providing an internationally accepted blueprint for sustainable development, pollution prevention and compliance assurance.
>
> Delmas Magali A., 2002

The most commonly adopted system in the UK is *ISO 14001*. This is an international standard which describes the requirements for an organization's EMS. It aims to provide organizations with the elements of an effective EMS that can be integrated with other management systems and contains requirements that can be objectively audited.

EMAS (Eco-Management and Audit Scheme) is a voluntary initiative designed to improve companies' environmental performance. It was initially established by European Regulation 1836/93, although this has been replaced by Council Regulation 1221/2009.

Its aim is to recognize and reward those organizations that go beyond minimum legal compliance and continuously improve their environmental performance. EMAS prescribes that participating organizations must:

- develop an environment policy;
- conduct an environmental review to identify its environmental impacts;
- develop a programme of actions to manage its identified environmental impacts;
- implement a management system which defines environmental responsibilities, environmental procedures and training programmes;
- conduct periodic environmental audits to assess environmental performance;
- produce a statement of environmental performance and make it available to the public; and
- seek external verification of the quality of environmental management from an independent accredited environmental verifier.

EMAS is often viewed as the most stringent management system, as there is an explicit requirement for legal compliance and reporting of this status to the regulator. (All other systems require identification of legislation relevant to an organization's activities, products and services and a commitment to assess the level of compliance against the identified legislation.) (See useful resources section for more information and links to EMS external certification schemes.)

The effectiveness of environmental management systems

The Northern Ireland Environment Agency commissioned a desktop study measuring the effectiveness of EMS in terms of improving environmental performance and reducing environmental impacts. This study concluded that there was 'strong evidence that EMS has a positive outcome in terms of improved environmental performance', but it was 'inconclusive' in terms of improvements in legislative compliance.[6] This review (in part) drew upon findings from a 2006 survey undertaken by ENDS, the Institute of Environmental

Management and Assessment (IEMA), the Environment Agency and the UK Accreditation Service which collated responses from more than 600 organizations. Seven in ten respondents said that implementing an EMS led to a 'significant environmental performance improvement that otherwise would not have been achieved'.[7] However, one in six (17 per cent) said EMSs made little difference to environmental performance, over and above that achieved by other drivers, while 13 per cent said they delivered only a short-term difference that was not sustained.

However, more recently findings from a study across the EU suggest that organizations adopting an EMS typically raise their environmental performance.[8] The researchers, from the Scuola Superiore Sant'Anna in Pisa, Italy, found a 'strong correlation between an organization incorporating an EMS and its ability to plan successfully and achieve its environmental targets'.

This study also found that enhanced environmental performance was linked to the length of time an EMS has been in place, despite the fact that these marginal gains diminish over time.

The study also looked at the impact on competitiveness and found that enhanced competitive performance was typically delivered if the EMS was fully integrated throughout an organization. Competitiveness was not, however, found to be improved by the length of time that an EMS had been in place. The main factor was the extent to which the EMS is embedded in the organization. The researchers concluded that 'even newly registered organizations could gain competitive benefits, provided the EMS was well implemented and managed'.

EMSs are also criticized for the fact that they do not consistently guarantee full compliance with environmental regulations, and that they only provide a framework within which an organization sets its own objectives. The absence of a 'clear accounting mechanism' and 'of mandatory reporting requirements' have also been identified as shortcomings in the ISO 14001 standard.[9] (Note that ISO 14001 is due to be reviewed and potentially revised in 2012.)

An organization may opt to have its EMS certified by an external assessor a
nd while this is not mandatory, gaining third-party recognition can help to demonstrate the organization's environmental responsibility to shareholders, the public, regulators, customers and clients. To ensure and demonstrate consistency and maintenance of standards, certification bodies can be accredited. In the UK, the relevant accreditation body is the UK Accreditation

Service (UKAS). Internationally, consistency among accreditation bodies is achieved through the International Accreditation Forum (IAF). This certification process has also come under fire and concerns with it have 'long been apparent'.[9] A 2003 survey conducted by ENDS and IEMA collated the responses of a sample of 350 ISO 14001-certified companies, consultancies and certification providers. Nearly one-half (48 per cent) felt that certification bodies were not sufficiently competent.[10] The follow-up survey conducted in 2006 indicated that doubts surrounding the certification process still remained.[11]

The effectiveness of social and ethical standards

'Audits have delivered some significant benefits. They have helped companies to map their supply chains, gain greater visibility of issues in the workplace, identify and deal with extreme forms of abuse, and make the workplaces safer and more hygienic. But on the negative side, commercial audits in particular, have delivered limited change for workers, do not provide reliable assurance about standards and add significant cost to the supply chain.'

Oxfam International, February 2010, 'Better Jobs in Better Supply Chains'[12]

Typically, organizations have relied heavily on codes of practice and on-site social audits, safe in the belief that they are doing the best they can to improve conditions for workers in their supply chains. But research from the Institute of Development Studies (IDS), which was commissioned by the Ethical Trading Initiative (ETI) to assess the impact and effectiveness of its base code (used by companies including Marks & Spencer, Tesco and GAP) revealed that more must be done in order to make a genuine difference. Over 400 workers in 23 supplier sites across the world were interviewed, as well as retailers, manufacturers, agents, managers, trade unions and non-governmental organizations (NGOs). The findings revealed that child labour, health and safety, and regular and overtime working hours had fallen as a result of implementation of the base code. However, in other areas the code had made little or no impact. Union membership showed no sign of increase in the sites visited and women were still denied basic equalities such as access to employment and training. Additionally, the codes made no progress in ensuring that workers received a living wage.[13]

Significantly, the research also suggested that observed reductions in the level of child labour were due to the enforcement of the law rather than the implementation of the codes.[13]

Neil Kearney, general secretary of the International Textile, Garment and Leather Workers' Federation, also argues that use of codes in some cases has worsened conditions in the supply chain. He gives, by way of example, the US Fair Labour Association's code of conduct, which stipulates that employees shall not be required to work more than 48 hours per week and 12 hours' overtime except in extraordinary business circumstances. This, he argues, gives the impression that a 60-hour week is acceptable. The ILO convention, on the other hand, clearly sets out that the working week should only exceed 48 hours in exceptional business circumstances.[13]

> The quality of auditing, in general, is very poor because of lack of training, lack of understanding, laziness or sometimes corruption.
>
> Neil Kearney, general secretary, ITGLWF[13]

> Buyers should not rely on documents from third party auditors to learn if a supplier is operating ethically, unless they know them well.
>
> David Ford, head of corporate social responsibility, Alfa Laval[14]

Auditing can be a time-consuming and expensive process and buyers need to understand that an audit is a snapshot in time, i.e. the day the auditor is on site. The quality of information will also depend on competence of the auditor. Checklist approaches to audits need to be used with caution; they can mean issues are not picked up and the legitimacy of this approach has been called into question with evidence of factories in Asia using sophisticated computer programs to create false books covering wage records and working hours.[13] For example, a supplier presented Oxfam with an audit report commissioned by a British retailer on a factory in China. The audit report found the factory to be 'compliant' with labour standards. Because of concerns about the reliability of the audit technique used, a more forensic assessment was commissioned involving off-site worker interviews. They found a range of serious problems, including child labour, wages below minimum levels and faked records.[15]

The impact of social audits on workers and businesses

From a worker's perspective	From a business perspective
Auditors focus on visible 'working conditions' rather than the broader 'employment conditions' (contract status, performance targets, and assumptions on overtime), which often matter more to workers	Audits do not provide assurance even against the worst forms of exploitation because of poor audit skills and methodology and increasing levels of fraud
Example: at one garment factory in Sri Lanka, an auditor set corrective action, stipulating a room where workers could eat and rest. However, in order to pay for these new facilities, the factory raised performance targets so high that workers didn't have time to use them.[16]	In the 98 sites assessed by Impactt, 45 per cent were found to have double books and 43 per cent coached workers to give the 'right answer'. In South East Asia the percentages were 83 per cent and 40 per cent.[17]
Typically 80 per cent of corrective actions relate to health and safety concerns; very few relate to issues such as freedom of association, a living wage, discrimination or harsh treatment (despite the importance of these to workers)	Audits add direct costs: recent World Bank research found that parallel (duplicate) audits in the Vietnamese garment industry cost approximately $50 per worker, per year. The need to protect commercial confidentiality has caused 'audit fatigue on a massive scale'
Many workers were not covered by audits as they were not formal employees	Audits add indirect costs: a corporate member of ETI estimated in 2006 that audits took up to 80 per cent of the time of ethical trade personnel

What else can I do to help assure responsible practices across my supply chains?

Many organizations are going 'beyond auditing' and focusing on what they need to do to help a supplier improve its social and environmental performance.

This may include providing suppliers with guidance on good practice and helping them keep up to date with economic, social and environmental legislation and appropriate industry standards. Training may also be provided to workers about their rights.

Collaboration with others, including companies, NGOs and industry bodies, can be useful for:

✓ commercial leverage for workplace and environmental improvements in your supply chain;
✓ harnessing expertise of organizations more familiar with bringing about such improvements; and
✓ finding collective solutions to problems. One company acting alone is unlikely to bring about change at an industry level but collaboration with other stakeholders can be a powerful voice.

Leading companies are also encouraging suppliers to move towards more mature systems of industrial relations which help to build suppliers' capacity for human resource management. They may also help to tackle public policy obstacles and provide public support for better enforcement of regulations to bring about change.

How you conduct your relationship with a supplier is also important; your purchasing practices affect conditions in the supply chain for better or worse. How suppliers are selected, lead times for orders, the types of relationship you have, contract terms and conditions and the way you deal with good or bad performance will all influence the way that suppliers manage their workforce and production methods. For example, the Ethical Trading Initiative (ETI) Impact Assessment in 2006: found that 'suppliers in all countries and sectors reported that [downward pressure on prices and lead times] limited their ability to make improvements in labour practices'.[18] Some poor purchasing practices result from inefficiencies (such as poor internal communication, late decision-making and frequent changes in product specifications), as well as from badly designed incentives and a lack of trusting business relationships. As such they are doubly undesirable: they both undermine labour standards and cost companies money.

In the report 'Better Jobs in Better Supply Chains' Oxfam recommends that you:

- Do fewer, better-quality audits, which include independent worker interviews and involve workers in setting and checking remedial actions.
- Work with local organizations that can also train workers on their rights; run a confidential helpline.
- Bridge the gap between corporate responsibility and sourcing staff; integrate ethics into supply chain management.
- Help turn the 'race to the bottom' to a 'level playing field founded on decent work' by distancing your company from lobbying to dilute labour regulations and by supporting civil society campaigns for effective enforcement.

© Oxfam International, February 2010, 'Better Jobs in Better Supply Chains'

The following table also outlines Oxfam's recommendations for benchmarking your company on labour standards.[19]

Step 1: Minimum expectations for an ethical sourcing programme

☐ Adopt a credible policy such as the ETI Base Code or SA8000 for consistent messaging to suppliers. These include standards which are vital to workers but which are left out of many codes.

☐ Decide the policy's scope, appoint a champion, invest in their learning, and adapt commercial terms to encourage continuous improvement in compliance. Communicate the policy and business case to stakeholders.

☐ Map supply chains, visit key production sites, minimize duplication of auditing, and prioritise corrective actions that matter to workers.

☐ Do no harm: don't cut and run when extreme forms of exploitation are exposed; don't lobby for the dilution of labour regulation.

Step 2: Signs of good practice

☐ Enhance your understanding of good practice by joining a multi-stakeholder initiative, treat NGOs as 'critical friends', and communicate learning throughout the business.

- ☐ Use best-practice audits involving workers for high-risk strategic suppliers, and check that there are at least a health and safety committee and a confidential helpline. Monitor workers' contract status and set targets to improve job security.
- ☐ Train buyers to understand their impact on workers and develop supplier relationships. Use a balanced scorecard and well-designed incentives. Rationalize the supply base and practise joint sourcing to overcome 'bottlenecks'.
- ☐ Be transparent. Report publicly on your labour standards activities and their impacts.

Step 3: Signs of leadership

- ☐ Publicly champion Ethical Trade as well as support Fairtrade, and lobby for a level business playing field based on effective enforcement of labour rights.
- ☐ Work with others to promote mature industrial relations and address the root causes of intractable issues, ensure workers are trained on their rights, partner with NGOs, and consider access agreements with unions.
- ☐ Select suppliers likely to observe the code, build their capacity, and reward them with longer contracts and fewer audits. Build a living wage into cost negotiations.
- ☐ Report progress against indicators that matter to workers, including awareness of rights, contract status and wages.

© Oxfam International, February 2010, 'Better Jobs in Better Supply Chains'

Summary

Codes of practice and standards do play a role in establishing requirements; they send a consistent message to suppliers and use of audits and third-party verification can help to gain assurance of business practices within your supply chains. However, they are not the whole answer. Social audits can help you to map supply chains, gain greater visibility of the issues in the workplace, identify and deal with more extreme forms of abuse and make the workplace safer and more hygienic. Standards, codes of practice and results of audits/external assessment are also useful as a basis for discussion with suppliers and workers, and can help to establish baselines from which change can be monitored. However, the quality of any related auditing and the competence of assessors is essential and research by respected NGOs recommends that fewer, better-quality audits should take place and social audits should include independent worker interviews and involve workers in setting and checking remedial actions.

For the most vulnerable supply chains, organizations need to move beyond social auditing and get involved with initiatives that address issues at a deeper and more fundamental level. How we behave as buyers is also important: we must ensure that lead times and pricing policies do not lead to excessive overtime or other socially or environmentally unsustainable practices. Buyers must critically examine their practices across vulnerable supply chains and strive to understand the impact of these practices on the suppliers' ability to meet their standards.

The benefits of good practice should help all parties not just the workers or communities affected by those supply chains. The purchasing organization stands to benefit, as demonstrating good practice may enhance (or protect) your brand image and reputation, differentiate you from competition, improve supplier relations and will help demonstrate transparency to stakeholders. The supplier can benefit by attracting new customers, longer-term contracts, improved worker morale, productivity and lower staff absenteeism and turnover.

Useful resources

'Win/Win: Achieving Sustainable Procurement with the Developing World'. Chartered Institute of Purchasing and Supply and Traidcraft, 2009. Available at: www.traidcraft.co.uk/Resources/Traidcraft/Documents/PDF/tx/ policy_report_win-win_Buyers_Guide.pdf

'Better Jobs in Better Supply Chains'. Oxfam International, February 2010. Available at: www.oxfam.org/en/policy/better-jobs-better-supply-chains

'Buying Your Way into Trouble: The Challenge of Responsible Supply Chain Management'. Insight Investment and Acona (2004)

Ethical Trading Initiative

ETI Base Code, Principles of implementation, 'Getting smarter at auditing', briefing paper (2006); 'Secrets and Lies' (DVD about audit fraud)

The ILO has a helpdesk to assist companies in aligning operations with international labour standards; email assistance@ ilo.org. The ILO–IFC 'Better Work Programme' (www.betterwork.org) provides remedial training to factories to improve compliance and competitiveness.

Gangmasters Licensing Authority (www.gla.gov.uk) – regulates labour providers in UK agriculture industries

Audit-related information sources

Supplier Ethical Data Exchange: www.sedex.org.uk

Fair Factories Clearinghouse: www.fairfactories.org

Local Resources Network: www.localresourcesnetwork.net

Ergon Associates and Dutch Sustainable Trade Initiative (2009) 'Beyond Auditing: Tapping the Full Potential of Labour Standards Promotion'.

Business for Social Responsibility (2007) 'Beyond Monitoring: A New Vision for Sustainable Supply Chains'

Social Auditor Standards Program: www.verite.org, sponsored by the US Department of State

Environmental management systems are a systematic, planned approach to the management of environmental issues at an organization and should be adopted as part of the overall company management structure. They are based on a plan–do–check–act methodology that aspires to continual improvement. There are a number of differing types of EMS. These can be summarized as:

- EMAS (Eco-Management and Audit Scheme) – see www.iema.net/ems/ emas?lang=_e
- BS EN ISO 14001 (International standard) – see www.bsigroup.co.uk/ en/Assessment-and-Certification-services/Management-systems/ Standards-and-Schemes/ISO-14001/
- BS 8555:2003 – see http://shop.bsigroup.com/en/ProductDetail/ ?pid=000000000030077920

- Acorn Scheme (phased approach) – see www.iema.net/ems/acorn_scheme/ bs8555?lang=_e
- Green Dragon (Arena Network) (phased approach) – see www.groundworkinwales.org.uk/greendragon/index.html.

The first four schemes can be subject to UKAS-accredited certification, and Green Dragon can be subject to UKAS-accredited inspection.

References

1 BS 8903 is a guidance standard. This means it provides advice but does not specify exacting requirements capable of being audited.
2 SA8000 is a global social accountability standard for decent working conditions, developed and overseen by Social Accountability International.
3 'Diageo: Vendor Ethics Are Main Supply Risk', *Supply Management*, 20 September 2010. Retrieved from: www.supplymanagement.com/news/2010/ diageo-vendor-ethics-are-main-supply-risk/?locale=en
4 Are We Forgetting about CSR? *Supply Management*, 6 August 2009.
5 *Mapping Sustainable Production in Ghanaian Cocoa*. Report by Cadbury and IDS. Retrieved from http://collaboration.cadbury.com/ourresponsibilities/ cadburycocoapartnership/Pages/mappingsustainableproduction.aspx
6 'Measuring the Effectiveness of Environmental Management Systems – Phase 1: Desktop Report', June 2009. Retrieved from: www.ni-environment.gov.uk/ measuring_the_effectiveness_of_ems_phase_1-2.pdf
7 ENDS Report 382, November 2006, pp.30–3. Retrieved from: www.endsreport.com/ 16518
8 *Journal of Cleaner Production*, 17, Issue 16 (November 2009), 1444–1452. F. Iraldo, F. Testa and M. Frey. 'Is an environmental management system able to influence environmental and competitive performance? The case of the eco-management and audit scheme (EMAS) in the European Union'.
9 EMS Frameworks up for review. ENDS Directory. Retrieved from www.endsdirectory.com/index.cfm?action=articles.view&articleid=201003
10 ENDS Report Issue 347, December 2003, pp.19–21. Retrieved from: www.endsreport.com/23272
11 ENDS Report Issue 382 November 2006, pp.30–33. Retrieved from: www.endsreport.com/16518/ems-survey-brings-mixed-news-for-certifiers

12 'Better Jobs in Better Supply Chains', Oxfam International, February 2010. Retrieved from: www.oxfam.org/en/policy/better-jobs-better-supply-chains[a]

13 'Purer Source', Emma Clarke, *Supply Management*, 4 January 2007. Retrieved from: www.supplymanagement.com/analysis/features/2007 /purer-source/?show=recent

14 'Audits Crucial to Supplier Wellbeing', Supply Management Web news, 5 June 2008. Retrieved from: www.supplymanagement.com/news/2008/ audits-crucial-to-supplier-wellbeing/?locale=en

15 'How to Address Labour Issues in Your Supply Chain – Tips And Examples', Oxfam GB, 2009. Retrieved from: www.oxfam.org.uk/resources/issues/privatesector/better-business.html

16 Interview with a garment worker and trade unionist in a Sri Lankan export-processing zone factory, by Thalia Kidder, 2003, of Oxfam GB.

17 Ethical Trading Initiative DVD (2007) 'Secrets and Lies' or Impactt

18 'Do Workers Really Benefit? Report on the Impact Assessment for Ethical Trading Initiative', S. Barrientos and S. Smith (2006) Institute of Development Studies, University of Sussex. Retrieved from www.ethicaltrade.org/ resources/key-etiresources/eti-impact-assessment

19 (For a more detailed set of benchmarks, go to: www.ethicaltrade.org/resources/ key-eti-resources/management-benchmarks.)

[a] The material on pages 154, 156 and 158–159, from 'Better Jobs in Better Supply Chains', 2010, is reproduced with the permission of Oxfam GB, Oxfam House, John Smith Drive, Cowley, Oxford OX4 2JY, UK www.oxfam.org.uk. Oxfam GB does not necessarily endorse any text or activities that accompany the materials.

10. How do I measure sustainable procurement performance?

Introduction

One of the biggest challenges to sustainable procurement lies in understanding what impact your actions and your suppliers' actions will have. Understanding what to measure and how to measure it is key. 'What you measure is what you get', so it's important to get this right. Getting the measures wrong can lead to perverse behaviour. For example, rapid-response paramedics may meet stated NHS targets and get to serious incidents in 8 minutes. However, if they are alone, they can only do a limited amount for the patient; if the patient dies, the target is still met. Arriving in 9 or more minutes, with more support, may mean that the patient lives; either way the target is still missed.

A robust methodology can be applied, but if it's measuring the wrong thing, then it's meaningless. To make sustainable procurement measures meaningful they need to be used in the context of achieving your stated sustainability objectives which should be aligned with (and contribute to) your higher-level organizational corporate sustainability goals.

Too often sustainability requirements are included in the tender, but little attention is paid to monitoring and measuring sustainable outcomes once the contract becomes operational. Issues also exist at an organizational level, for example, the report *Accounting for Sustainability* (2007) found that 'reporting of sustainability performance is inconsistent and often overcomplicated and inaccessible'.[1] Leading organizations are now working hard to understand how best to measure and report sustainability performance to give a more balanced and complete picture of overall company performance. This means ensuring that broader and longer-term sustainability considerations are integrated and connected with traditional accounting measurements.

This chapter examines different types of measures and provides some advice on how to develop meaningful measures. The final section of this chapter will examine reporting and provide some summary hints and tips for better measurement.

What is performance measurement and why is it needed?

Performance measurement can be described as 'the process of developing measurable indicators that can be systematically tracked to assess progress made in achieving predetermined goals' (GAO).[2]

> An indicator is something that helps you understand where you are, which way you are going and how far you are from where you want to be. A good indicator alerts you to a problem before it gets too bad and helps you recognize what needs to be done to fix the problem.
>
> Source: www.sustainablemeasures.com

It is important to note that there is a difference between an 'indicator' and a 'key performance indicator' (KPI).

A KPI can be defined as a pre-agreed measure (whether qualitative or quantitative) of performance against objectives of an organization. These are the indicators that really matter and the number should be limited; if you have many KPIs, then by definition they cannot all be key. Typically, these will be supported by a series of indicators which help measure your progress in achieving those important KPIs. To avoid confusion, it is probably better to refer to those performance indicators as measures. The following example should help illustrate this point:

✍ London 2012 Olympics – athletes are in a programme of four years' preparation; there is only one KPI – the Olympic Gold medal. As an athlete how do you know if your training and preparation are getting you there? If you are a runner, you do weights, sprints, laps, and so on … building strength, stamina, speed, you measure heart rate before and after, recovery times, lung capacity and so on … none of these are the end goal, but they are measures of progress in getting to the final test. One KPI, lots of measures, so measures are about 'fitness'.

Measurement helps us:

✓ assess our progress in achieving stated goals;
✓ understand what impact we are having whether positive or negative;
✓ learn from our successes and failures; and
✓ acquire information needed to make decisions.

Types of measures

Measurement of sustainable procurement will have both qualitative and quantitative dimensions and may be applied to both purchasing practices and outcomes. Typically, sustainability measures can be divided into three areas.

1 **Management measures**: these tend to reflect procurement/departmental practices. As an organization's maturity and competence of sustainable procurement increases, these tend to evolve into more tangible operational-level measures.

Examples of such practice measures are:

➢ percentage of contracts awarded based on WLC criteria;
➢ percentage of contracts awarded based on MEAT (most economically advantageous tender) criteria;
➢ level of flexible framework achieved;
➢ percentage of contracts with sustainability criteria included (or percentage value of contracts);
➢ number of supply chain staff trained in sustainable procurement;
➢ supplier performance criteria – e.g. number of suppliers meeting their sustainability targets;
➢ number of red (i.e. high)-inherent sustainability risks on risk register/number of red-residual sustainability risks on risk register; and
➢ percentage of audits carried out for high-risk supply chains.

These are typically a 'measure of inputs' rather than a 'measure of outcomes' and their limitations need to be understood; for example, measuring the use of sustainability clauses in contracts offers poor protection in the event of a major environmental or child labour issue. Also, some of these practice measures become redundant as organizations move from development to operation. For example, United Utilities stopped measuring Flexible Framework progress after two years when it had achieved all it wanted and moved towards more outcome-based measures.

2 **Operational measures**: these tend to be more focused on the actual outcomes of sustainable initiatives, for example, actual reduction in waste sent to landfill, reduction in carbon emissions, water usage, increases in recycled content, etc. Table 9 provides a good example of use of outcome-based measures and targets; it is a comprehensive overview of the

sustainable procurement objectives and targets associated with construction and staging of the 2012 Olympics.

3 **Environmental condition measures**: these are more macro-economic measures that are not typically used at the supply chain level. However, some organizations might use such indicators to inform overall strategy. An example could be use of concentrations of air contaminants associated with motor vehicle emissions which may be used to inform an organization's transport or fleet policy.

Single indicators are unlikely to measure the efficiency of the various aspects of sustainable procurement and organizations typically use a small number of indicators covering both inputs and outcomes.

The Flexible Framework

The Flexible Framework (which was introduced in Chapter 4) is one of the most commonly used tools to measure sustainable procurement progress over time. It is a practice measure which is widely used across the public sector. This self-assessment tool was designed so that it could be used by all organizations: from those with significant levels of procurement expertise and resource to those with very limited resource at their disposal. (See useful resources section for more links to information on using the Flexible Framework.)

Developing meaningful measures

> The trouble with measurement is its seeming simplicity.
>
> Source unknown

The process of measuring may not seem difficult, but deciding what to measure and how to measure is. In the words of Albert Einstein 'Not everything that counts can be counted and not everything that can be counted counts'.

Table 9 – London 2012 sustainable procurement objectives/targets for construction and staging of the Olympic and Paralympic Games

	Construction-related targets	Games-related targets
Carbon	➢ **Energy efficiency** of buildings: all buildings to be 15% more energy efficient than current building regulations ➢ Reduction in **carbon emissions** achieved above 2006 building regulations: target 50% reduction ➢ Energy from **renewables**: 20% energy demand to come from renewables post Games ➢ All buildings to be rated BREEAM excellent ➢ All cooling systems HFC free	➢ **Olympic fleet: cars with fleet average emissions of 120g/km** ➢ Logistics carbon footprint: baseline to be calculated and improved ➢ Use of low embodied materials ➢ **20% electricity from renewable resources during the Games**
Water	➢ **Water usage**: permanent venues and non-residential buildings to reduce water demand by 40% compared with average ➢ 20% reduction in water usage of residential buildings compared with London average	
Waste	➢ **Reuse/recycling**: at least 90%, by weight, of the demolition material to be reused/recycled ➢ **Reuse/recycling**: at least 90%, by weight, of the construction material to be reused/recycled ➢ **Reuse/recycling**: reasonable endeavours to achieve 90%, by weight, of post-Games material and equipment to be reused/recycled	➢ **Zero waste to landfill during Games** ➢ **Reuse/recycling**: reasonable endeavours to achieve 90%, by weight, of post-Games material and equipment to be reused/recycled

	Construction-related targets	Games-related targets
Materials	➢ **Responsible sourcing**: 100% timber used from known, legal sources, with clear supply chain evidence ➢ At least 20% of **construction materials**, by value, to be from a reused or recycled source ➢ Achieve a level of 25% recycled aggregate, by weight, for the permanent venues and associated Olympic Park-wide infrastructure	➢ Responsible sourcing: 100% timber used from known, legal sources, with clear supply chain evidence ➢ Paper and card should be produced using non-chlorinating bleaching methods and aim to achieve 75% post-consumer recycled content for coated paper, and 100% post-consumer waste for uncoated paper. Any virgin fibre used must be from FSC-certified sources ➢ Maximize recycled content, compliance with packaging guidelines ➢ Compliance with WEEE and RoHS directives
Biodiversity and ecology	➢ **Ecological management plans** in place for all stages of construction	➢ **Ecological management plans for all venues**
Land, air, water, noise	➢ **Environmental management plans**: 100% of tier-one constructors to have plans in place. Tier-two suppliers to operate own plans or work within tier-one contractors' plans ➢ **Considerate constructors scheme (CCS)**: all contractors required to register for the CCS, and achieve a score of at least four in each section of the scheme	➢ **Environmental management plans for all venues**

	Construction-related targets	Games-related targets
Supporting communities	➤ **Programme of community engagement**	➤ ETI base code for labour standards ➤ 100% workers to receive London Living Wage on site ➤ Use of Fairtrade Labelling Organizations International (FLO), the Soil Association organic certification, the Rainforest Alliance, or other appropriate standards ➤ Get Set programme for schools ➤ Changing places programme for communities
Transport and mobility	➤ **Construction material transport**: at least 50% of materials, by weight, to be transported to the Park by rail and water during construction	➤ Low emissions transport plans for cars and bus services
Access	➤ **Lifetime Homes Standards**: Village to be built in accordance with this standard post-Games ➤ 10% of the housing will be fully wheelchair accessible post-Games	➤ **Accessibility plans for all venues**
Employment and skills	➤ 15% employees resident in five host boroughs ➤ 7% employees previously unemployed ➤ 2,000 apprenticeships ➤ 3 skills centres established for construction skills	➤ 3 skills centres established for catering, customer service and security

How do I measure sustainable procurement performance?

	Construction-related targets	Games-related targets
Health and well-being	➤ Delivery against H&S standards ➤ Use of hazardous substances ➤ Phthalate-free PVC	➤ Delivery against H&S standards ➤ Use of hazardous substances ➤ No PVC materials purchased ➤ No animal-tested products without approval ➤ Animal welfare standards for catering ➤ No materials from ICUN red list of threatened species ➤ London 2012 Food Vision ➤ Restrictions on use of heavy metals and brominated fire retardants
Inclusion	➤ 15% women in construction jobs on site ➤ 30% employees of black, Asian and minority ethnic (BAME) origin ➤ 5% disabled employees ➤ Use of 'CompeteFor' in procurement	➤ Suppliers sign up to diversity and inclusion business charter ➤ Suppliers required to use 'Diversity works for London' standard ➤ Use of 'CompeteFor' in procurement

Retrieved from:

www.london2012.com/documents/oda-publications/oda-sustainable-development-strategy-executive-summary.pdf

www.london2012.com/documents/locog-publications/sustainable-sourcing-code.pdf

www.london2012.com/documents/business/diversity-and-inclusion-business-charter.pdf

Meaningful measures enable you to understand progress towards your goals and should tell you something that you don't already know. The following advice may help you develop meaningful measures:

- Objective – measures should be objective, independent and neutral (i.e. independent of politics and other agendas).
- Strategic – measures must be developed and used in the context of achieving stated objectives. Sustainable procurement measures should be relevant and linked to organizational sustainability strategies and objectives, i.e. this should ensure that procurement is aligned with the organization's

sustainable development aspirations, creating a 'golden thread' back to the core purpose of the business.
- Suitable – good measures should be quantifiable and capable of being expressed as a performance indicator.
- Available – the organization or supply chain should be able to provide the required information.
- Prioritized – you should know what your most important measures are.
- Time-bound – measures should be time-bound; any timescales need to be both realistic and achievable.

It is not appropriate to prescribe what and how an organization should measure its sustainable procurement activity and outcomes. No single measurement approach is best: organizations will have different objectives which will require different measures and methodologies. There is no one-size-fits-all approach. However, to provide a balanced overview of sustainable procurement performance you should try to adopt a suite of measures which includes consideration of the social, economic and environmental aspects of sustainable procurement. The 2009 report *Measurement of Sustainable Procurement* examined methodologies for measuring sustainability within public sector procurement; it concluded that 'using a smart KPI approach' provided the most practical way forward. This enables different methodologies to be used to measure different indicators meaning the three dimensions of sustainable development (economic, social and environmental) can be adequately covered. This report also suggested that for each dimension of sustainable development there are likely to be a small number of generic or corporate-level indicators that should occur in almost all procurements and then also a larger number of performance indicators that are specific to the particular procurement and the sustainable priorities related to that procurement.[3]

Organizations have traditionally measured their procurement success on economic measures, predominantly cost savings achieved. However, over the past 10 to 15 years the use of environmental measures has also grown as a way of measuring procurement performance. The use of social measures tends to be less mature and many organizations look at social indicators simply as risk mitigation. This is a good first step but measuring the social impact is becoming more important. Social measures aim to address the 'less tangible' impacts on communities and individuals within or affected by an organization's supply chains. These measures need to be quantifiable and objective, yet sensitive enough to capture the key social issues and benefits for those individuals or communities.

How do I measure sustainable procurement performance?

> ### Example
>
> Nokia publically reports on the environmental performance of its supply chain. As at 31 December 2009, 92 per cent of direct suppliers' sites serving Nokia were certified to environmental management system (EMS) standard ISO 14001. In 2009 Nokia increased the visibility of suppliers' environmental performance and target setting, concentrating on four key areas:
>
> 1   energy consumption;
> 2   carbon dioxide (equivalent) emissions;
> 3   water consumption; and
> 4   waste generation.
>
> Of the suppliers deemed to have the highest sustainability impacts, 93 per cent have company-level reduction targets covering these key areas. (This represents 70 per cent of hardware expenditure.)
>
> From a social perspective suppliers are expected to have a company-level code of conduct in place. Codes of conduct set out requirements in several areas, such as corruption, general business routines, health and safety, human rights, working conditions, social rights and environmental standards. In 2010 Nokia was working on developing additional social indicators to provide a more comprehensive picture of social performance of its direct supply chain.
>
> Source: Form 20–F– 2009. Retrieved from: www.nokia.com/NOKIA_COM_1/About_Nokia/Financials/form20-f_09.pdf

Social Return on Investment (SROI) is an emerging area for procurement. This attempts to measure value created by a project (or organization or policy) in its broadest terms. It aims to measure social, environmental and economic outcomes that do not normally have market values and attempts to place a financial value on them. The aim is to provide a means of ensuring that all values are considered in decision making which is normally based on financial data. For example, if the building of a community centre had an aim of regenerating an area by employing unemployed people, we could measure the actual number of people employed. However, SROI would then take that figure and seek to calculate a value for it. For example, the amount saved on state benefits and income tax generated is a direct and objective measure. However, SROI would potentially ascribe more 'softer' values than these direct values. For example, we know that people in employment cost less to the NHS and they commit less crime.[4] SROI generates a monetary value for these kinds of indirect outcomes.[6] However these figures are not true cash savings and therefore are neither objective nor directly quantifiable. This in practical terms alone renders them unlikely to be effective as meaningful measures'.[3]

LM3 (Local Multiplier 3) is another emerging indicator worth mentioning. This is a local multiplier tool which was created by the New Economics Foundation. It aims to determine how money coming into your community is then spent and re-spent. It is intended for any person or organization who sees a need for measuring the impact of aspects of local spending in their communities. LM3 aims to help you understand how much local spending benefits the community.

Selecting and implementing sustainable procurement measures

Sustainable procurement measures should be informed by your organization's stated sustainability objectives/CSR intentions. Aligning sustainable procurement objectives and measures with these higher-level goals is important and demonstrates the contribution that good procurement can make. To do this you will need to have a good understanding of what your organization's objectives are and why they are important to the business. Remember that organizations have unique drivers and different reasons to be sustainable; therefore, all organizations have unique sustainable goals. For example, Interserve, the support services and facilities management company, has identified ten corporate-level sustainable priorities which it has incorporated into a framework – RENEWABLES (see Figure 21). Each of these sustainable themes is represented by one letter within the word and has enabled all staff to understand what sustainability means to Interserve and what its priorities are. This has helped procurement to shape its sustainability objectives and provides clear direction for buyers around the sustainability requirements that its supply chain is expected to deliver on.

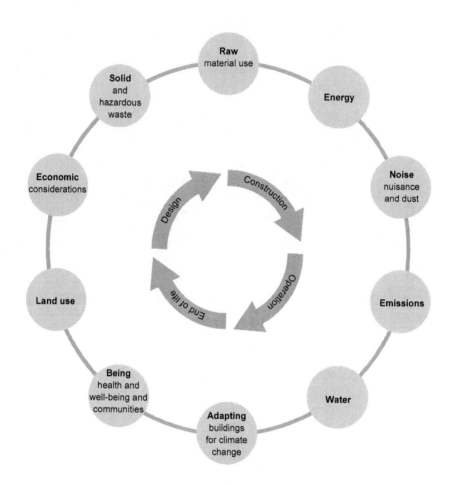

Figure 21 – Interserve renewables framework
(© 2010 Interserve)

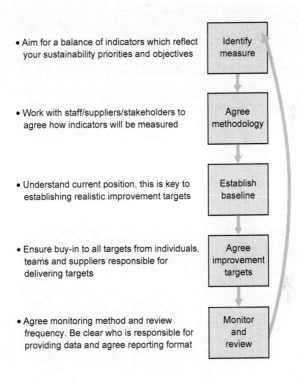

• Aim for a balance of indicators which reflect your sustainability priorities and objectives → **Identify measure**

• Work with staff/suppliers/stakeholders to agree how indicators will be measured → **Agree methodology**

• Understand current position, this is key to establishing realistic improvement targets → **Establish baseline**

• Ensure buy-in to all targets from individuals, teams and suppliers responsible for delivering targets → **Agree improvement targets**

• Agree monitoring method and review frequency. Be clear who is responsible for providing data and agree reporting format → **Monitor and review**

Figure 22 – Implementing measurement – key steps

How do I measure sustainable procurement performance?

Before relevant sustainable procurement measures can be set, it is important that the scope and boundaries of your sustainable objectives are clearly defined, i.e. it is important to know what is meant by the objective, what's included and what's not included. For example, United Utilities (UU) identified and defined 12 key supply chain sustainability risks and impacts that it requires its buyers to manage as part of their ongoing supply chain management activities. They have clearly defined what is meant by each impact and established scope and boundaries of each impact which has maintained clarity and alignment for purchasing staff and enabled consistent measures to be set. Waste to Landfill is one of the 12 impacts, which is defined as 'only waste sent to landfill as a result of the company's own activities, including construction, operational and office-based activities. Supplier's waste from manufacture and waste that does not arise from UU's own organization is not included'.

Figure 22 illustrates the basic steps involved when developing performance indicators and corresponding targets.

The following table illustrates UU's supply chain sustainability targets; these are based on the 12 sustainability impacts that the organization has identified as important. These targets cover a six-year period as UU has recognized that affecting the supply chains will take time as both buyer and supplier sustainable business skills are developed. (Note UU updates these targets periodically; targets shown are valid as at August 2010.)

Area	Year 09/10	Year 10/11	Year 11/12	Year 12/13	Year 13/14	Year 14/15
Energy	50% procurement decisions based on UU energy impact 30% procurement actions demonstrate energy reduction	80% procurement decisions based on UU energy impact 50% procurement actions demonstrate energy reduction 1 forward commitment made to marketplace	100% procurement decisions based on UU energy impact 50% procurement actions demonstrate energy reduction 2 forward commitments made to marketplace	1 forward commitment delivered 3 forward commitments made to marketplace	2 forward commitments delivered 4 forward commitments made to marketplace	3 forward commitments delivered 5 forward commitments made to marketplace
CO_2			30% carbon-intensive supply reporting footprint to point of manufacture	50% carbon-intensive supply reporting footprint to point of manufacture 30% renewable energy purchased for UU	50% carbon-intensive supply reporting footprint to point of manufacture 10% delivering carbon reductions	50% carbon-intensive supply reporting footprint to point of manufacture 20% delivering carbon reductions 10% carbon-intensive reporting footprint back to raw materials
Materials		30% suppliers reporting on sensitive and recycled materials	70% suppliers reporting on sensitive and recycled materials. 50% supply to good industry standard practice (Wrap, WWF, etc.) and reduction targets 5 examples of reuse	90% suppliers reporting on sensitive and recycled materials. 70% supply to good industry standard practice (Wrap, WWF etc.) and reduction targets 10 examples of reuse	90% suppliers reporting on sensitive and recycled materials 90% supply to good industry standard practice (Wrap, WWF, etc.) and reduction targets 15 examples of reuse	

Area	Year 09/10	Year 10/11	Year 11/12	Year 12/13	Year 13/14	Year 14/15
Waste to landfill	70% suppliers reporting on waste sent to landfill	90% suppliers reporting on waste sent to landfill; 30% suppliers have waste to landfill reduction targets; 1 forward commitment made to marketplace	2 forward commitments made to marketplace	90% suppliers reporting on waste sent to landfill; 50% suppliers have waste to landfill reduction targets; 30% suppliers can demonstrate reductions made; 1 forward commitment delivered; 3 forward commitments made	2 forward commitments delivered; 4 forward commitments made to marketplace	90% suppliers reporting on waste sent to landfill; 90% suppliers have waste to landfill reduction targets; 50% suppliers can demonstrate reductions made; 3 forward commitments delivered; 5 forward commitments made
Air emissions			50% of engines in operation conform to good industry standard practice (e.g. Euro CAT 4)		75% of engines in operation conform to good industry standard practice (e.g. Euro CAT 4)	90% of engines in operation conform to good industry standard practice (e.g. Euro CAT 4)
Hazardous substances		30% suppliers with risk evaluations		75% of suppliers with risk evaluations; 50% with no residual red risks > mitigation		90% of suppliers with risk evaluations; 90% with no residual red risks > mitigation
Biodiversity	30% of construction projects have biodiversity action plan	30% suppliers with risk evaluations	50% of construction projects have biodiversity action plan	75% of suppliers with risk evaluations; 50% with no residual red risks > mitigation	75% of construction projects have biodiversity action plan	90% of suppliers with risk evaluations; 90% with no residual red risks > mitigation

Water			10% water-intensive supply reporting footprint to point of manufacture	25% water-intensive supply reporting footprint to point of manufacture	50% water-intensive supply reporting footprint to point of manufacture; 10% delivering water reductions	75% water-intensive supply reporting footprint to point of manufacture; 20% delivering water reductions; 10% water-intensive reporting footprint back to raw materials
Emissions to water	30% suppliers with risk evaluations			75% of suppliers with risk evaluations; 50% with no residual red risks > mitigation		90% of suppliers with risk evaluations; 90% with no residual red risks > mitigation
Fair treatment	>75% suppliers correctly presented supplier invoices paid on time	£100K of new business with SME – tier two and below	>80% of correctly presented supplier invoices paid on time	£200K of new business with SME – tier two and below	>90% of correctly presented supplier invoices paid on time	£300K of new business with SME – tier two and below
Labour standards	Supply chain labour standards/code of conduct communicated effectively by June 2009 (to meet Dow Jones)	30% of suppliers with risk evaluations		75% of suppliers with risk evaluations; 50% with no residual red risks and press briefing, i.e. after mitigation		90% of suppliers with risk evaluations; 90% with no residual Red risks and press briefing, i.e. after mitigation

Area	Year 09/10	Year 10/11	Year 11/12	Year 12/13	Year 13/14	Year 14/15
Education		30% suppliers with risk evaluations		75% of suppliers with risk evaluations 50% with no residual red risks > mitigation		90% of suppliers with risk evaluations 90% with no residual red risks > mitigation
Employment	30% suppliers with risk evaluations		75% of suppliers with risk evaluations 50% with no residual red risks > mitigation		90% of suppliers with risk evaluations 90% with no residual red risks > mitigation	

The Sustainable Procurement Guide

Translating sustainable procurement targets into supplier requirements and performance targets

Typically, procurement will set departmental-level sustainable performance targets as illustrated by the UU example above. These targets will normally include a combination of practice and operational indicators. It is the role of the buyer to then translate any targets that are relevant into specific supplier requirements and performance improvement targets within the tender process and ongoing supplier management activity. Figure 23 illustrates this linkage.

Not all supplier sustainability requirements may be delivered by the tender and captured in the resulting contract. For example, it may be an emerging issue that is not well understood, such as embodied water, or be a longer-term aspirational requirement of the organization. Other sustainability requirements may emerge as a result of an ongoing risk assessment that runs in parallel with the procurement process, or legislative changes may also drive changes in sustainability requirements. Suppliers are not bound to deliver on any sustainability requirements, measures or improvement targets that are not written into the contract; however, often suppliers understand the benefits

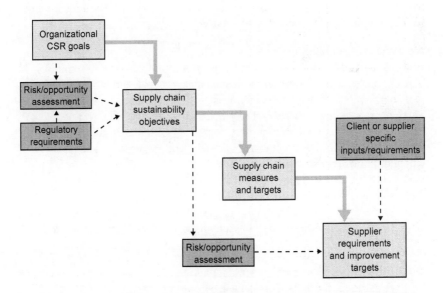

Figure 23 – Development of supplier sustainability requirements, measures and targets

and can be persuaded to embrace sustainability initiatives and performance targets on a voluntary basis. Note that baseline-data gathering might be required before meaningful measures can be jointly agreed with suppliers. This may be more complicated or time-consuming than it first appears. For example, a major airport operator attempted to set targets for buying certified timber and timber products, but this took some time, as initially it didn't understand the current position, including where the timber was sourced from.

Reporting on sustainability

The buyer and supplier should jointly agree the timescales and procedures for reviewing performance and progress towards improvement targets. Where possible, this should be incorporated into existing processes and suppliers should report on their progress towards more sustainable practices and outcomes alongside other indicators such as service, quality, technical and cost performance. A balanced scorecard approach is often used to present overall performance.

Gaining a consistent approach to reporting a supplier's progress makes it easier and more efficient to report departmental performance which should contribute to reporting of overall company performance.

More and more organizations have begun to publicly report their performance towards sustainability. Wal-Mart is a high-profile example and has ambitious plans to measure and report on the sustainability of every product it sells. This sustainability index initiative aims to measure product sustainability in four areas: energy and climate, natural resources, material efficiency, and people and community. The consortium group established (involving universities, retailers, suppliers and NGOs) has an ambitious agenda, and has created a series of working groups that aim to create a common set of sustainability measurement and reporting standards for various sectors and product categories. It also plans to develop an online 'Sustainability Information Hub', containing a library of such standards.[5] For the world's largest retailer to be taking sustainability this seriously suggests how important this agenda is and how it is perceived to be linked to future commercial success.

This trend towards increased transparency and reporting can mean suppliers are being asked to report on sustainability in similar but different ways and there is increasing recognition that a move towards more consistent and common measures and methodologies would improve efficiency for all involved. The

Carbon Disclosure Project (CDP) supply chain programme provides an example. This is a collaboration of global corporations that have extended their climate change and carbon management strategies to engage with their suppliers via CPD's annual information request. Member companies use CPD's standardized format to communicate with their suppliers in a streamlined, unified annual request.

The Sustainability Reporting Framework developed by the Global Reporting Initiative (GRI) is another example of a reporting framework that has been developed to provide a more consistent and efficient approach. GRI is a non-profit network, consisting of thousands of stakeholders worldwide that build and enhance the Framework together. The Framework, which is freely available to the public, supports organizations in defining report content and enables easy comparison of performance of various organizations, or within organizations over time. It also acknowledges the uniqueness of every organization and its circumstances. Therefore, guidance includes opportunities for each organization to add its own performance indicators in its communications.

The Connected Reporting Framework has also been developed to help to provide clearer, more consistent and comparable information for use both within an organization and externally. This model also aims to illustrate the interconnected nature of an organization's actions. (See useful resources section for links to more information on these frameworks.)

Summary

Presenting a balanced understanding of your supply chain's contribution to more sustainable business practices is important, but providing meaningful indicators can be difficult to achieve. The following checklist summarizes the most important issues.

- All sustainable procurement measures must be set in context, particularly around the organization's strategy/CSR goals. Critically, it is this strategy which should determine what is measured and reported.
- The shape and nature of measures will change by industry and by company depending on the business model and key drivers of value.
- Try to use standard measures where possible to make reporting more efficient for suppliers and enable easier comparison of information.

How do I measure sustainable procurement performance?

- Ensure measures provide a balanced picture of progress across economic, social and environmental aspects of sustainable procurement. Practice and operational measures are normally required.
- Qualitative and quantitative measures may be required; qualitative measures are often more appropriate for measuring the social context.
- Ensure that all measures tell you something meaningful – if not, don't bother!
- Measures should not be 'set in stone'; measures should be reviewed and adjusted as the sustainable agenda and your organizational objectives evolve.

> The only man who behaved responsibly was my tailor, he took my measurement every time he saw me, while all the rest went on with their old measurements and expected them to fit me.
>
> George Bernard Shaw

- Ensure that you understand the baseline position, as this is vital to agreeing appropriate targets.
- Any information reported externally should align with information reported internally; if it's not used internally, then it should not be reported externally.
- If you have more than 12 KPIs, they are probably not all 'key'.

Useful resources

Global Reporting Initiative, Sustainable Reporting Framework, see: www.globalreporting.org

Accounting for Sustainability, Connected Reporting Framework (CRF), see: www.sustainabilityatwork.org.uk/strategy/report/0

BT provides a good example, demonstrating how corporate responsibility can be measured and reported. This example illustrates the use of a range of financial and non-financial indicators. It also follows the principles of the CRF. See: www.btplc.com/Responsiblebusiness/Ourstory/Sustainabilityreport/Keyperformanceindicators/index.aspx

LM3 – The Money Trail – 'Measuring Your Impact on the Local Community Using LM3', see: www.neweconomics.org/publications/money-trail

Social Return on Investment (SROI), see www.thesroinetwork.org

Flexible Framework

Defra Flexible Framework Guidance for Public sector organizations, see: www.defra.gov.uk/sustainable/government/advice/public/buying/documents/flexible-framework-word-guidance.pdf

Action Sustainability Flexible Framework Online Assessment Tool, see www.actionsustainability.com/evaluation/flexible_framework

Sustainable business practice benchmarking and indices

Dow Jones Sustainability Indexes are global indexes tracking the financial performance of the leading sustainability-driven companies worldwide, see: www.sustainability-index.com

FTSE4Good is designed to measure the performance of companies that meet globally recognized corporate responsibility standards, and to facilitate investment in those companies. See: www.ftse.com/Indices/FTSE4Good_Index_Series/index.jsp

Business in the Community's CR Index is a UK-based voluntary benchmark of Corporate Responsibility (CR). It helps companies to integrate and improve CR throughout their operations by providing a systematic approach to managing, measuring and reporting on business impacts in society and on the environment. See: www.bitc.org.uk/integration_and_advice/index.html

References

1   *Accounting for Sustainability*, 2007. Retrieved from: www.sustainabilityatwork.org.uk
2   GAO–US Government Accountability Office. Retrieved from: www.gao.gov/special.pubs/bprag/bprgloss.htm

3 'Measurement of Sustainable Procurement', Adam Wilkinson and Bill Kirkup, September 2009. Retrieved from: www.actionsustainability.com/news/212/Measurement-of-sustainable-procurement/

4 Unemployment and Ill Health: Local Labour Markets and Ill Health in Britain 1984–1991. *Work, Employment & Society*, September 1999, 13: 461–482.

5 Walmart Sustainability Index, see http://walmartstores.com/Sustainability/9292.aspx

11. What does the future hold?

Introduction

The sustainable agenda is constantly evolving as our knowledge, experience and competence grows. This final chapter takes a look at the future of sustainable procurement, discussing potential trends, issues and business practices that are now starting to emerge. It begins by taking a look at what is on the horizon for sustainable procurement and then goes onto examine the bigger picture, including how leading organizations are embracing sustainable development across the wider value chain; the evolving role of NGOs; and how the next generation will respond to the sustainability challenges they will undoubtedly inherit.

On the horizon?

It is impossible to predict with any certainty how this agenda will evolve. At a macro-economic level we don't yet know what the commercial implications of the near double-digit growth being experienced in some of the Asian countries, such as China, India and Korea, will be. As these countries become less competitive and developed economies respond, will the trend towards offshoring become less popular and globalization possibly be slowed in favour of economic localization? Economic localization occurs when a region, county, city – even a neighbourhood – frees itself from overdependence on the global economy and invests in local resources to produce a significant portion of the goods, services, food and energy it consumes. A strategy that brings production of vital goods and services close to home is arguably more environmentally, economically and socially sustainable than a strategy based on economic globalization and will certainly have major implications on the way we buy and how we manage our supply chains. There are some early signs that this may gain momentum, for example, the Bay Area Economic Localization Campaign is under way to localize the San Francisco Bay Area economy by promoting small, locally owned, environmentally sustainable businesses in the energy, food, manufacturing and financial sectors.[1]

Taking a more focused view of sustainable procurement over a shorter-time horizon, current signals suggest that the following factors are likely to become more prominent.

What does the future hold?

The role of assurance – continued demand for greater transparency and verification across supply chains is likely to motivate companies to reassess the extent of independent assurance and public accountability required. The ODA is leading the way here having established the Commission for a Sustainable London 2012 which provides independent assurance to the Olympic Board and the public on how the bodies delivering the Games and its legacy are meeting their sustainability commitments.

This assurance is also unique in that it is inherently forward looking. It is not possible to look backwards at an Olympics and say how you would do it better next time. Given that many organizations are setting forward-looking sustainability objectives it is necessary to develop a more forward-looking approach to assurance, possibly based on the Commission model. For example, Marks & Spencer's Plan A now looks forward to 2016, so does the government target to deliver zero carbon homes by 2016. The process to evaluate suppliers' capability to develop towards *future* objectives has not been invented at the time of writing this book but it is anticipated to be a very important development as the principle of sustainable procurement develops and matures.

In conjunction with assurance, the trend towards more international and better standards is likely to continue.

Collaboration – sustainability is not a single issue but a series of issues that are all interrelated. Making progress not only requires commitment at a company level but industry-level action (or greater) may be required. For example, many electronics organizations have come together alongside the Global e-Sustainability Initiative (GeSI) and the Electronic Industry Citizenship Coalition (EICC) to overcome challenges around the supply of metals for use in the electronics industry. This includes the ability to trace and track the sources of metals and the industry's ability to influence conditions.

To maximize progress we need to share learnings and collaborate. In short, this is an agenda where organizations can and should co-operate.

Innovation and new technology – will continue to provide a way to improve our social and environmental progress through smarter ways of conducting our activities. Improving living standards alongside population growth will put a heavy weight on the planet and technological innovation will continue to play a vital role in moving towards more sustainable business practices and more sustainable solutions.

Organizations are increasingly recognizing the need to create the right business environment which can harness supply chain expertise, foster innovation, move fast and take 'considered' risk. The market is already responding, as illustrated by 'Green Dragons', which at the time of writing is being launched by Action Sustainability. This is a subscription-based service to create a continuous 'sustainable innovation pipeline' for a small group of construction clients. This service goes beyond the normal strategic sourcing and into more innovative supply chain development. The proposition will involve selecting and grooming the best potential innovations over a period of several years to ensure that subscribing partners gain competitive advantage through access to the very best innovations. This will also provide societal benefits in terms of competitiveness of UK plc, jobs, economic growth, 'green economy', etc.

Legislation and policy – new and emerging legislation will continue to shape the sustainable procurement agenda. The most notable, recent legislation is the Equality Act 2010 and the Climate Change Act 2008.

> **Equality Act 2010** – sets out new laws which aim to help narrow the gap between rich and poor and create a more equal society in the UK. It aims to simplify the law which, over the last four decades, has become complex and difficult to navigate. Nine major pieces of legislation and around 100 other measures have been replaced by a single Act written in plain English to make it easier for individuals and employers to understand their legal rights and obligations. At the time of writing, the Equality Act has not been completely enforced (the first wave of implementation was 1 October 2010), its provisions coming into force at different times to allow time for the people and organizations affected by the new laws to prepare for them and to ensure that the Act is implemented in an effective and proportionate way.

The Equality Act measures include:

- introducing a new public sector duty to consider reducing socio-economic inequalities;
- putting a new Equality Duty on public bodies;
- using public procurement to improve equality;
- introducing gender pay and equality reports;
- extending the scope to use positive action;
- banning age discrimination outside the workplace;
- strengthening the powers of employment tribunals;
- protecting carers from discrimination;

- protecting breastfeeding mothers;
- banning discrimination in private members' clubs; and
- strengthening protection from discrimination for disabled people.

The Act encourages public bodies to promote equalities and diversity through their procurement. (Public bodies spend over £220 billion a year. That gives them a lot of buying power which can be used to encourage suppliers to treat people fairly in the way they do their work.) There are already some examples of good practice in this area from Transport for London and the London 2012 project, both of whom expect their suppliers to have diversity action plans to support their work for the client. LOCOG, the Olympic Games operator, requires all suppliers to take part in the Diversity Works for London scheme.[2]

It is early days for this new legislation in terms of the impact it may have on businesses but it could be profound. Businesses may need to move away from a passive 'equal opportunities' approach to a more proactive strategy for equality. For example, organizations may be required to regularly review gender pay differences and publish the results, and in terms of the supply chain suppliers may be required to have proactive strategies to deal with diversity. The pre-qualification process may need to reflect this, and organizations may be required to work with long-term suppliers to help improve their approach to diversity, using schemes like Diversity Works for London.[2]

Finally, it is important to create the right organizational culture where people are prepared to be open about their minority status. Those businesses that fail to be positive about minorities may miss an opportunity to attract talented people or competitive suppliers. This legislation should not be seen as a burden; rather, good businesses should embrace it as a reason to increase the relentless search for talent and competitive suppliers.

➢ **Climate Change Act 2008** – makes the UK the first country in the world to have a legally binding long-term framework to cut carbon emissions. The target of at least an 80 per cent cut in greenhouse gas emissions by 2050 is to be achieved through action in the UK and abroad. Also, a reduction in emissions of at least 34 per cent by 2020 must be achieved. Both these targets are against a 1990 baseline.

Supply chains account for a large share of global carbon emissions and procurement can make a real difference by reducing the amount of carbon expended in the manufacture and delivery of goods and services throughout the supply chain.

For example, the NHS Sustainable Development Unit published a report examining the sources of its 18 million tonne annual carbon footprint. The result outlined in 'NHS England Carbon Emissions: Carbon Footprinting Report' was that, while energy use made up 22 per cent of total emissions, and travel 18 per cent, the other 60 per cent was generated by procurement (defined in this case as the purchase of goods and services through the supply chain by the NHS in England).[3]

The Carbon Reduction Commitment (recently renamed the CRC Energy Efficiency Scheme) was launched in April 2010 and affects about 5,000 private and public sector organizations with an annual energy spend greater than £500,000.[4] This involves monitoring emissions use, and the purchase of permits to release CO_2 emissions initially at £12 per tonne of CO_2 and after 2012 at a price determined by auction. Many purchasers do not consider the amount their organizations have to pay for emissions to be onerous; as a result it is unlikely to make a significant difference initially. But Chris Bowden, chief executive of energy procurement consultancy Utilyx, advises buyers to be cautious. He indicates that eventually a global agreement on carbon emissions will be reached; it will just take time and that the cheap carbon prices today are unlikely to stay cheap in the longer term.[5]

Government policy, such as the UK Sustainable Construction Strategy, and legislation, such as the Climate Change Act, tend to focus primarily on operational energy consumption and not on the embodied impacts described in Scope 3 of the Greenhouse Gas Protocol. As legislation drives down the energy in the use of buildings, vehicles and other products, the energy used to make them will become more important. A small number of leading organizations already know this and are working with their supply chains to define, measure and reduce these impacts, but most are not. This growing trend will become more important and enlightened leaders need to start to address this issue.

Water – is also an emerging issue. While earth is a water wealthy planet, only a tiny portion of its water is available to support people and aquatic species. Changes in water availability will occur as a result of temperature increases, population growth and increasing industrialization. It is estimated that by 2050, one-third of the people on earth may lack a clean, secure source of water.[6] It is also surprising to learn how much water is embedded in the production of everyday products. For example, 1kg of beef requires 13,620 litres of water to produce,[7] a pair of leather shoes requires approximately 8,000 litres of water[8] and a cotton shirt requires 2,900 litres[6] of water. Water usage and the water footprint of our supply chains (i.e. the amount of water embodied in the production of goods and services purchased within our supply chains) is likely to come under increasing scrutiny as parts of the planet experience greater 'water stress'. We will also see a greater focus on water management and conservation to meet the demands of growing populations and expanding economies while still ensuring protection for the diversity of life that water sustains.

The trend towards greater environmental awareness has been due to a number of factors, including growing scientific evidence, government policy, international collaboration, standards and legislation. This has led to some organizations behaving more responsibly over the past 40 years or so. The international environmental NGOs have driven this agenda through a combination of campaigning, research and direct action. Organizations such as WWF, Greenpeace and Friends of the Earth are household names in many parts of the world.

Social NGOs and awareness of the social injustice generated by irresponsible behaviour at the top of the supply chain are far less prominent today but this is likely to change. The media today tends to make heroes of swashbuckling business leaders who drive down prices, cut out waste and behave ruthlessly with their employees and suppliers. As the impact of this type of behaviour becomes more well known, consumers and ethical investors will make more responsible choices, driven by an increasingly prominent population of social NGOs.

Beyond sustainable procurement

We should also look beyond the limits of procurement and consider some wider issues that may influence the sustainability landscape. We are already seeing that some organizations are now starting to look beyond their supply chains to influence the wider sustainability agenda. Are there things that we are doing now that will unknowingly create problems in the future? Could certain assets today become liabilities in the future? Also, how will the role of NGOs evolve, and how are the next generation going to think and act? This section will take a brief look at some of these wider issues and considerations which may well help to shape decision making in the future.

Managing sustainability across the wider value chain

Sustainable procurement is inherently focused on sustainable sourcing, responsible management of the supply chain and the practices of suppliers participating within those supply chains. However, some leading companies are going further and not only managing sustainability of suppliers lower down the supply chain but are taking responsibility across the whole value chain in an attempt to make it more sustainable. Marks & Spencer, using its Plan A sustainability programme, has been mentioned earlier in this book. Marks & Spencer decided to take responsibility for impacts related to the way its customers wash, dry and iron their clothes. This redefined the relationship between retailer and customer; it also gave rise to supply chain innovations in low-temperature wash products, and non-iron and low tumble-dry garments.

A lesser-known example is in the oil and gas sector. FMC Technologies Ltd launched its 'Greenshoots Fund' in 2009 which is an innovative scheme designed to partially mitigate the environmental impact resulting from the manufacture, sale and distribution of its core product – large installations known as subsea trees placed below sea level and used in the extraction of oil and gas.

Shaun McCarthy explains:

> The scheme works by creating a fund to pay a shadow price for carbon related to air travel and the energy embodied in every stage of the manufacturing process. The money is used to invest in local projects which save carbon and deliver some local economic benefit. Although launched very recently the scheme has had a profound effect. FMC's customers, who contribute to the fund to mitigate their embodied carbon emissions, have become more carbon aware and will demand more information about the emissions related to products they buy. Suppliers asked to supply more carbon information are already questioning the efficiency of some of their manufacturing processes, reducing costs and emissions. FMC has also gained planning consent to build a 1.5MW wind turbine to power their main premises in Scotland. In future, suppliers able to demonstrate a similarly responsible attitude will be rewarded with more business.

> The ultimate vision is for the Greenshoots fund to be redundant because the whole value chain is of such low carbon it is not necessary. In the medium term it acts as a stimulus for customers, manufacturers and suppliers to focus on this issue while doing some good for society in the local community.[9]

The role of NGOs

NGOs have played a significant role in driving us towards more sustainable business practices and are set to remain a powerful stakeholder group that will help to shape the sustainability agenda. Today there is a lot of focus on climate change, but where will their future focus lie?

Environmental NGOs and social NGOs have a tendency to act differently; the explanation probably lies in their history. A number of environmentally focused NGOs have been around for a long time and as such their approach has 'matured' with less extreme direct action and a less confrontational approach towards major business organizations. In future it's likely that the NGOs' relationship with business will evolve further and we may possibly see more integration with business, as is the case with WWF's One Planet Initiative. This initiative involves WWF working in partnership with corporations and business leaders to provide conservation benefits and support in shaping a more sustainable global economy. (For more information, see http://wwf.panda.org/what_we_do/how_we_work/businesses.)

Some former NGOs have also evolved with more commercial consultancy offerings: for example, the Carbon Trust and Forum for the Future now both offer commercial consultancy services. Either way, NGOs are here to stay. Many are set to remain powerful, well-supported organizations that businesses are wise to engage if they are serious about making real positive changes which will shape our future sustainability performance.

The next generation

Maintaining progress towards more sustainable business practices and society calls for an explicit consideration of future generations. Youth will inherit many of the environmental, economic and social problems created over the past decades and incorporating their opinions and concerns is key to continued progress. Schools are embracing the sustainability agenda especially on the environmental side and the next generation should more fully understand the impact that their lifestyles and consumer choices will have on society and the environment. Successful organizations will be the ones that are capable of understanding how the next generation will think and act and then aligning themselves with these new demands and changed behaviours.

> Young people should be at the forefront of global change and innovation. Empowered, they can be key agents for development and peace. If, however, they are left on society's margins, all of us will be impoverished. Let us ensure that all young people have every opportunity to participate fully in the lives of their societies.
>
> Kofi Annan

How young people will make their employment choices is also likely to change. There is already increasing evidence to show that today's students have to feel happy with the ethical behaviour of a prospective employer before accepting a job. To encourage the best young talent into our organizations we will have to demonstrate responsible practices and values. FMC Technologies has been quoted throughout this book as an example of good practice. Its managing director is adamant that his primary motivation is people related. There has been a trend away from the most talented graduates going into engineering or wishing to work in the oil and gas industry. By differentiating the company as being innovative around sustainability, he firmly believes that this will help to win the battle to attract and retain the talent that is needed to maintain its market-leading position. This example of leadership is in short supply and more is needed to engage with tomorrow's generation of responsible business leaders.

We should also spare some thought for the serious social problems emerging among the more disadvantaged young people in our society. For example, youth unemployment is recognized as a serious societal problem which has other repercussions on social welfare, inclusion, health and crime. The work environment provides opportunities for learning, developing social contacts, self-reliance and economic security that is often a prerequisite for partnership formation and parenthood. The capacity of leaders and organizations to address this issue and provide young people with the opportunities and skills needed by employers will be critical to creating a successful, inclusive society.

Summary

The sustainability agenda is constantly evolving and we will never have perfect knowledge or any certainty about what the future agenda will look like. Twenty years ago we were all worried about the ozone layer and as a result HFCs were invented to replace CFCs and HCFCs (ozone-depleting substances). However, HFCs still have very high global warming potential (2,000 times that of CO_2) and so in solving one problem we were still contributing to another one, which at the time we knew very little about. Another example is the replacement of oil used in high-voltage switch circuit breakers in power stations with Sulphur Hexafloride (SF_6) gas. Oil was replaced because of environmental problems around disposal, but SF_6 is the most potent greenhouse gas that the Intergovernmental Panel on Climate Change has evaluated (it has a global warming potential that is 23,900 times worse than CO_2!) and has its own disposal problems. We don't yet understand how some of our actions today may be creating future environmental problems. Similarly, what we consider assets today may become potential liabilities in the future. Take, for example, an organization that leases commercial buildings: today its largest assets, i.e. fully air-conditioned buildings with little thermal insulation, could potentially become a liability as clients increasingly demand green, energy-efficient buildings that promote the health and well-being of their employees.

Successful organizations will continue to take sustainability seriously as they recognize that profit, big business and sustainability can work together. This is exemplified by the successful commercial partnerships that LOCOG (the government-owned private company responsible for staging the 2012 Olympic and Paralympic Games) has formed with its commercial sponsors.

LOCOG has worked hard, ever since the bid, to make sustainability an integral part of the London 2012 brand; the appointment of the independent sustainability Commission helps to reinforce this commitment. To be associated with such a brand is attractive to sponsors that want to develop their green credentials and to offer high levels of sustainability. 'This starts to create a virtuous cycle of sustainability between partners and gives rise to some amazing deals', says Shaun McCarthy, chairman of the Commission for a Sustainable London 2012.[10]

Examples include the partnership with Adidas, which LOCOG trust to manage labour standards well, which has provided a significant proportion of sponsorship and licensing revenue. AdiZones, which have been created in each of the host boroughs to provide community sports facilities, are also a result of this relationship. Low-emission cars from BMW and the provision of adapted cars for disabled drivers for the first time in Olympic history are other good examples.[10]

> Good procurement can act as the catalyst for sustainable development and procurement/commercial teams can act as gatekeepers.
>
> Shaun McCarthy, chairman of the Commission for a Sustainable London 2012

To summarize, there is no trade-off between sustainability and commercial success; the sustainability agenda is here to stay and forward-thinking organizations will continue to embrace the opportunities and provide leadership. We must continue to embed sustainability into our decision making and business practices and in the words of William James:

Act as if what you do makes a difference. It does.

References

1   See: www.rprogress.org/sustainable_economics/economic_localization.htm for more information
2   Diversity Works for London offers two Equality & Diversity Standards, both tailored to meet the needs of business of all sizes and sectors. For more information, see: www.diversityworksforlondon.com.
3   'NHS England Carbon Emissions: Carbon Footprinting Report'. Retrieved from: www.sd-commission.org.uk/publications.php?id=816
4   See www.carbonreductioncommitment.info/ for more information
5   'Climate of Change', Andy Allen, Supplymanagement.com, 7 January 2010. Retrieved from: www.supplymanagement.com/analysis/features/2010/climate-of-change
6   'Freshwater', *National Geographic*. Retrieved from: http://environment.nationalgeographic.com/environment/freshwater
7   'The Hidden Water We Use', *National Geographic*. Retrieved from: http://environment.nationalgeographic.com/environment/freshwater/embedded-water/
8   'Reducing the Impact of Humanity's Water Footprint, WWF. Retrieved from: http://wwf.panda.org/what_we_do/footprint/water/
9   'Managing Sustainable Value Chains', Shaun McCarthy, September 2009. Retrieved from: www.actionsustainability.com/news/208/Managing-sustainable-value-chains-
10 'A Sporting Chance of Sustainability', *Public Servant*, June 2010, p.41.